Gluten-Free Cookbook for Beginners

Over 365 Days of Quick and Simple Recipes for Delicious Meals in 30 Minutes or Less

By

Olivia James

Copyright © 2023 Olivia James
All rights reserved.

No part of this book may be reproduced or used in any manner without the written permission of the copyright owner, except for the use of quotations in a book review and certain other non-commercial uses permitted by copyright law.

- **ISBN :** 978-0-6459126-0-9 **(print)**
- **ISBN:** 978-0-6459126-1-6 (eBook)

Table of Contents

GLUTEN FREE BREAKFAST RECIPES 5

- Recipe 1: Gluten-Free Banana Pancakes 5
- Recipe 2: Gluten-Free Veggie Omelette 5
- Recipe 3: Gluten-Free Berry Chia Pudding 6
- Recipe 4: Gluten-Free Quinoa Salad with Lemon-Herb Dressing 6
- Recipe 5: Gluten-Free Avocado Toast 7
- Recipe 6: Gluten-Free Stir-Fried Chicken and Vegetables 7
- Recipe 7: Gluten-Free Berry Smoothie Bowl 8
- Recipe 8: Gluten-Free Mexican Quinoa Stuffed Peppers 8
- Recipe 9: Gluten-Free Spinach and Feta Omelette Cups 9
- Recipe 10: Gluten-Free Thai Peanut Chicken Stir-Fry 10
- Recipe 11: Gluten-Free Blueberry Muffins 10
- Recipe 12: Gluten-Free Quinoa Salad with Lemon-Herb Dressing 11
- Recipe 13: Gluten-Free Banana Bread 12
- Recipe 14: Gluten-Free Quinoa Fried Rice 12
- Recipe 15: Gluten-Free Overnight Oats 13
- Recipe 16: Gluten-Free Chicken and Vegetable Stir-Fry 13
- Recipe 17: Gluten-Free Zucchini Fritters 14
- Recipe 18: Gluten-Free Chicken and Vegetable Curry 15
- Recipe 19: Gluten-Free Chocolate Chia Pudding 15
- Recipe 20: Gluten-Free Shrimp Stir-Fry with Vegetables 16
- Recipe 21: Gluten-Free Banana Pancakes 17
- Recipe 22: Gluten-Free Chicken Stir-Fry with Broccoli and Cashews 17

GLUTEN-FREE LUNCH RECIPES 19

- Recipe 1: Quinoa Salad with Roasted Vegetables 19
- Recipe 2: Thai Chicken Lettuce Wraps 19
- Recipe 3: Smashed Avocado Chickpea Salad Sandwich 20
- Recipe 4: Spinach and Feta Stuffed Chicken Breast 20
- Recipe 5: Cauliflower Fried Rice 21
- Recipe 6: Caprese Quinoa Stuffed Peppers 21
- Recipe 7: Tuna and Avocado Lettuce Wraps 22
- Recipe 8: Greek Salad with Grilled Chicken 22
- Recipe 9: Zucchini Noodles with Pesto 23
- Recipe 10: Quinoa Black Bean Salad 24
- Recipe 12: Mexican Quinoa Stuffed Bell Peppers 25
- Recipe 13: Shrimp Stir-Fry with Vegetables 25
- Recipe 14: Quinoa Spinach Stuffed Mushrooms 26
- Recipe 15: Egg Salad Lettuce Wraps 26
- Recipe 16: Mediterranean Chickpea Salad 27
- Recipe 17: Thai Peanut Zucchini Noodles 27
- Recipe 18: Baked Turkey Meatballs with Marinara Sauce 28
- Recipe 19: Quinoa Stuffed Butternut Squash 29
- Recipe 20: Avocado Tuna Salad Wraps 29
- Recipe 21: Cauliflower Fried Rice with Shrimp 30
- Recipe 22: Caprese Chicken Salad 30

- RECIPE 23: SWEET POTATO AND BLACK BEAN QUESADILLAS 31
- RECIPE 24: GREEK CHICKEN PITA POCKETS 32
- RECIPE 25: QUINOA STUFFED AVOCADO BOATS 32

GLUTEN-FREE DINNER RECIPES 33
- RECIPE 1: GARLIC LEMON CHICKEN WITH ROASTED VEGETABLES 33
- RECIPE 2: SHRIMP STIR-FRY WITH RICE NOODLES 33
- RECIPE 3: QUINOA STUFFED BELL PEPPERS 34
- RECIPE 4: ZUCCHINI NOODLE STIR-FRY WITH CHICKEN 34
- RECIPE 5: BAKED SALMON WITH LEMON DILL SAUCE 35
- RECIPE 6: SPINACH AND FETA STUFFED CHICKEN BREAST 35
- RECIPE 7: BEEF AND BROCCOLI STIR-FRY 36
- RECIPE 8: SPAGHETTI WITH TOMATO BASIL SAUCE 37
- RECIPE 9: THAI GREEN CURRY WITH VEGETABLES 37
- RECIPE 10: MEDITERRANEAN QUINOA SALAD 38
- RECIPE 11: EASY CHICKEN AND VEGETABLE STIR-FRY 38
- RECIPE 12: ZESTY LIME SHRIMP TACOS 39
- RECIPE 13: CAPRESE CHICKEN SKILLET 39
- RECIPE 14: QUINOA STUFFED BELL PEPPERS 40
- RECIPE 15: SALMON AND ASPARAGUS FOIL PACKETS 40
- RECIPE 16: TERIYAKI BEEF STIR-FRY 41
- RECIPE 17: TOMATO BASIL ZUCCHINI NOODLES 42
- RECIPE 18: STUFFED PORTOBELLO MUSHROOMS 42
- RECIPE 19: THAI BASIL CHICKEN STIR-FRY 43
- RECIPE 20: GREEK SALAD WITH GRILLED CHICKEN 43
- RECIPE 21: QUINOA STUFFED BUTTERNUT SQUASH 44
- RECIPE 22: PESTO CHICKEN WITH ROASTED VEGETABLES 44
- RECIPE 23: MEXICAN QUINOA STUFFED PEPPERS 45
- RECIPE 24: LEMON GARLIC SHRIMP SKEWERS 46
- RECIPE 25: BAKED LEMON HERB SALMON 46
- RECIPE 26: QUINOA AND VEGETABLE STIR-FRY 47
- RECIPE 27: ZUCCHINI NOODLES WITH TOMATO SAUCE 47
- RECIPE 28: HONEY MUSTARD CHICKEN WITH ROASTED VEGETABLES 48
- RECIPE 29: QUINOA STUFFED MUSHROOMS 48

GLUTEN-FREE DESSERT RECIPES 50
- RECIPE 1: CHOCOLATE MUG CAKE 50
- RECIPE 2: STRAWBERRY SPINACH SALAD 50
- RECIPE 3: HONEY GLAZED SALMON 51
- RECIPE 4: QUINOA STUFFED BELL PEPPERS 51
- RECIPE 5: APPLE CINNAMON OATMEAL 52
- RECIPE 6: CAPRESE SKEWERS 52
- RECIPE 7: CHICKPEA SALAD 52
- RECIPE 8: GLUTEN-FREE BANANA PANCAKES 53
- RECIPE 9: MEDITERRANEAN QUINOA SALAD 53
- RECIPE 10: GLUTEN-FREE LEMON BARS 54
- RECIPE 11: QUINOA STIR-FRY 55

GLUTEN-FREE SEAFOOD RECIPES 56

RECIPE 1: LEMON GARLIC SHRIMP	56
RECIPE 2: BAKED SALMON WITH HERB CRUST	56
RECIPE 3: GRILLED GARLIC BUTTER PRAWNS	57
RECIPE 4: THAI COCONUT CURRY SHRIMP	57
RECIPE 5: GRILLED LEMON HERB SEA BASS	58
RECIPE 6: BAKED COD WITH TOMATO AND OLIVE SALSA	58
RECIPE 7: GARLIC LIME GRILLED PRAWNS	59
RECIPE 8: GRILLED CAJUN SHRIMP SKEWERS	59
RECIPE 9: BAKED LEMON HERB SALMON	60
RECIPE 10: BAKED GARLIC HERB SCALLOPS	60
RECIPE 11: TUNA AVOCADO LETTUCE WRAPS	61
RECIPE 12: PAN-SEARED HALIBUT WITH LEMON BUTTER SAUCE	61
RECIPE 13: GLUTEN-FREE SHRIMP STIR-FRY	62

GLUTEN-FREE SIDE DISH RECIPES 63

RECIPE 1: ROASTED GARLIC PARMESAN BRUSSELS SPROUTS	63
RECIPE 2: LEMON GARLIC QUINOA	63
RECIPE 3: HONEY GLAZED CARROTS	64
RECIPE 4: GARLIC PARMESAN QUINOA	64
RECIPE 5: BALSAMIC ROASTED VEGETABLES	65
RECIPE 6: HERBED QUINOA SALAD	65
RECIPE 7: ZUCCHINI FRITTERS	66
RECIPE 8: GARLIC ROASTED CAULIFLOWER	66
RECIPE 10: SWEET POTATO WEDGES	67
RECIPE 11: LEMON HERB ROASTED POTATOES	68
RECIPE 12: GRILLED ASPARAGUS WITH LEMON AND PARMESAN	68
RECIPE 13: CUCUMBER TOMATO SALAD	69
RECIPE 14: ROASTED GARLIC CAULIFLOWER MASH	69
RECIPE 15: BAKED PARMESAN ZUCCHINI FRIES	70

GLUTEN-FREE VEGETABLE RECIPES 71

RECIPE 1: ROASTED GARLIC AND HERB CAULIFLOWER RICE	71
RECIPE 2: ZUCCHINI NOODLES WITH TOMATO AND BASIL	71
RECIPE 3: SWEET POTATO AND CHICKPEA CURRY	72
RECIPE 4: SPINACH AND MUSHROOM QUINOA STIR-FRY	72
RECIPE 5: OVEN-ROASTED ROOT VEGETABLES	73
RECIPE 6: CAPRESE STUFFED PORTOBELLO MUSHROOMS	73
RECIPE 7: RAINBOW VEGGIE STIR-FRY	74
RECIPE 8: CHICKPEA AND VEGETABLE CURRY	75
RECIPE 9: ROASTED BRUSSELS SPROUTS WITH BALSAMIC GLAZE	75
RECIPE 10: QUINOA STUFFED BELL PEPPERS	76
RECIPE 11: GARLIC HERB ROASTED VEGETABLES	77

Gluten free Breakfast Recipes

Recipe 1: Gluten-Free Banana Pancakes
Cooking time: 15 minutes
Servings: 2
Ingredients:
- 2 ripe bananas
- 2 large eggs
- 1/2 cup gluten-free oat flour
- 1/2 teaspoon baking powder
- 1/4 teaspoon ground cinnamon
- Maple syrup, for serving
- Fresh berries, for garnish (optional)

Instructions:
1. In a mixing bowl, mash the bananas using a fork until smooth.
2. Add the eggs to the bowl and whisk until well combined.
3. In a separate bowl, mix together the oat flour, baking powder, and ground cinnamon.
4. Gradually add the dry ingredients to the banana and egg mixture, stirring until a smooth batter forms.
5. Heat a non-stick frying pan over medium heat and lightly grease it with oil or cooking spray.
6. Pour 1/4 cup of the batter onto the pan for each pancake. Cook for 2-3 minutes until bubbles appear on the surface.
7. Flip the pancakes and cook for an additional 1-2 minutes until golden brown.
8. Remove the pancakes from the pan and repeat the process with the remaining batter.
9. Serve the pancakes warm with a drizzle of maple syrup and fresh berries, if desired.

Nutrition information per serving (without syrup or berries):
- Calories: 256
- Protein: 10g
- Carbohydrates: 46g
- Fat: 5g
- fibre: 6g

Recipe 2: Gluten-Free Veggie Omelette
Cooking time: 20 minutes
Servings: 2
Ingredients:
- 4 large eggs
- 2 tablespoons milk
- Salt and pepper, to taste
- 1 tablespoon olive oil
- 1/4 cup diced bell peppers
- 1/4 cup sliced mushrooms
- 1/4 cup chopped spinach
- 2 tablespoons grated cheddar cheese

Instructions:
1. In a bowl, whisk together the eggs, milk, salt, and pepper.
2. Heat the olive oil in a non-stick frying pan over medium heat.
3. Add the bell peppers, mushrooms, and spinach to the pan. Sauté for 3-4 minutes until the vegetables are tender.
4. Pour the egg mixture over the sautéed vegetables in the pan.
5. Cook for 3-4 minutes, gently lifting the edges of the omelette with a spatula to allow the uncooked eggs to flow to the bottom.
6. Sprinkle the grated cheddar cheese evenly over the omelette.

7. Fold the omelette in half and continue cooking for an additional 1-2 minutes until the cheese is melted and the eggs are cooked through.
8. Slide the omelettes onto a plate and cut it in half to serve.

Nutrition information per serving:
- Calories: 212
- Protein: 14g
- Carbohydrates: 5g
- Fat: 15g
- fibre: 1g

RECIPE 3: GLUTEN-FREE BERRY CHIA PUDDING

Cooking time: 5 minutes (plus chilling time)
Servings: 2
Ingredients:
- 1 cup almond milk
- 1/4 cup chia seeds
- 1 tablespoon honey or maple syrup
- 1/2 teaspoon vanilla extract
- 1/2 cup mixed berries (such as blueberries, raspberries, and strawberries)
- 2 tablespoons chopped nuts (such as almonds or walnuts), for topping

Instructions:
1. In a bowl, whisk together the almond milk, chia seeds, honey or maple syrup, and vanilla extract.
2. Let the mixture sit for 5 minutes, then whisk again to prevent clumping.
3. Cover the bowl and refrigerate for at least 2 hours or overnight until the mixture thickens and becomes pudding-like in consistency.
4. Before serving, give the chia pudding a good stir.
5. Divide the pudding into serving bowls or glasses.
6. Top each portion with mixed berries and chopped nuts.
7. Serve chilled.

Nutrition information per serving:
- Calories: 225
- Protein: 6g
- Carbohydrates: 22g
- Fat: 13g
- fibre: 12g

RECIPE 4: GLUTEN-FREE QUINOA SALAD WITH LEMON-HERB DRESSING

Cooking time: 30 minutes
Servings: 2
Ingredients:
- 1/2 cup quinoa
- 1 cup water
- 1/2 cup diced cucumber
- 1/2 cup halved cherry tomatoes
- 1/4 cup chopped fresh parsley
- 2 tablespoons chopped fresh mint
- 2 tablespoons lemon juice
- 1 tablespoon olive oil
- Salt and pepper, to taste

Instructions:
- Rinse the quinoa under cold water to remove any bitterness.
- In a saucepan, combine the quinoa and water. Bring to a boil, then reduce the heat to low, cover, and simmer for 15-20 minutes until the quinoa is tender and the water is absorbed.
- Remove the quinoa from the heat and let it cool for a few minutes.

- In a large bowl, combine the cooked quinoa, diced cucumber, cherry tomatoes, parsley, and mint.
- In a small bowl, whisk together the lemon juice, olive oil, salt, and pepper to make the dressing.
- Drizzle the dressing over the quinoa salad and toss gently to combine.
- Adjust the seasoning if needed.
- Serve the salad at room temperature or chilled.

Nutrition information per serving:
- Calories: 256
- Protein: 7g
- Carbohydrates: 39g
- Fat: 8g
- fibre: 6g

RECIPE 5: GLUTEN-FREE AVOCADO TOAST

Cooking time: 10 minutes
Servings: 2
Ingredients:
- 2 slices gluten-free bread
- 1 ripe avocado
- Juice of 1/2 lemon
- Salt and pepper, to taste
- Optional toppings: sliced cherry tomatoes, crumbled feta cheese, red pepper flakes, fresh herbs (such as cilantro or basil)

Instructions:
1. Toast the gluten-free bread slices until golden and crispy.
2. In a small bowl, mash the ripe avocado with a fork.
3. Squeeze the lemon juice over the mashed avocado and season with salt and pepper to taste. Mix well.
4. Spread the avocado mixture evenly onto the toasted bread slices.
5. Add your desired toppings, such as sliced cherry tomatoes, crumbled feta cheese, red pepper flakes, or fresh herbs.
6. Serve immediately.

Nutrition information per serving:
- Calories: 214
- Protein: 5g
- Carbohydrates: 23g
- Fat: 13g
- fibre: 7g

RECIPE 6: GLUTEN-FREE STIR-FRIED CHICKEN AND VEGETABLES

Cooking time: 30 minutes
Servings: 2
Ingredients:
- 2 boneless, skinless chicken breasts, sliced into thin strips
- 2 tablespoons gluten-free soy sauce
- 1 tablespoon honey
- 1 tablespoon olive oil
- 1 garlic clove, minced
- 1 teaspoon grated fresh ginger
- 1 red bell pepper, sliced
- 1 small zucchini, sliced
- 1 cup broccoli florets
- Salt and pepper, to taste
- Optional garnish: sliced green onions, sesame seeds

Instructions:
1. In a small bowl, whisk together the gluten-free soy sauce and honey. Set aside.
2. Heat the olive oil in a large frying pan or wok over medium-high heat.

3. Add the minced garlic and grated ginger to the pan and cook for 1 minute until fragrant.
4. Add the sliced chicken to the pan and stir-fry until cooked through, about 5-6 minutes.
5. Add the sliced bell pepper, zucchini, and broccoli florets to the pan. Stir-fry for an additional 3-4 minutes until the vegetables are tender-crisp.
6. Pour the soy sauce and honey mixture over the chicken and vegetables. Stir well to coat everything evenly. Cook for 1-2 minutes until the sauce thickens slightly.
7. Season with salt and pepper to taste.
8. Remove from heat and garnish with sliced green onions and sesame seeds if desired.
9. Serve the stir-fried chicken and vegetables over cooked rice or quinoa, if desired.

Nutrition information per serving (excluding rice/quinoa):
- Calories: 280
- Protein: 30g
- Carbohydrates: 18g
- Fat: 10g
- fibre: 4g

RECIPE 7: GLUTEN-FREE BERRY SMOOTHIE BOWL

Preparation time: 10 minutes
Servings: 2
Ingredients:
- 2 ripe bananas, frozen and sliced
- 1 cup mixed berries (such as strawberries, blueberries, and raspberries), frozen
- sliced fresh berries, granola, shredded coconut, honey or maple syrup
- 1/2 cup almond milk (or any milk of your choice)
- 2 tablespoons chia seeds
- Toppings:

Instructions:
1. In a blender, combine the frozen banana slices, frozen mixed berries, almond milk, and chia seeds.
2. Blend until smooth and creamy, adding more almond milk if needed to achieve desired consistency.
3. Pour the smoothie mixture into serving bowls.
4. Top with sliced fresh berries, granola, shredded coconut, and drizzle with honey or maple syrup.
5. Enjoy immediately with a spoon.

Nutrition information per serving:
- Calories: 248
- Protein: 5g
- Carbohydrates: 52g
- Fat: 5g
- fibre: 11g

RECIPE 8: GLUTEN-FREE MEXICAN QUINOA STUFFED PEPPERS

Cooking time: 30 minutes
Servings: 2
Ingredients:
- 2 large bell peppers (any colour)
- 1/2 cup cooked quinoa
- 1/2 cup black beans, drained and rinsed
- 1/2 cup diced tomatoes
- 1/4 cup corn kernels (fresh or frozen)
- 1/4 cup chopped red onion
- 1/4 cup chopped fresh cilantro
- 1 teaspoon cumin
- 1/2 teaspoon chilli powder
- Salt and pepper, to taste
- Optional toppings: shredded cheese, avocado slices, sour cream, salsa

Instructions:

1. Preheat the oven to 375°F (190°C).
2. Cut the bell peppers in half lengthwise, removing the seeds and membranes.
3. In a mixing bowl, combine the cooked quinoa, black beans, diced tomatoes, corn kernels, red onion, cilantro, cumin, chilli powder, salt, and pepper. Stir well to combine.
4. Spoon the quinoa mixture evenly into each bell pepper half, pressing it down gently.
5. Place the stuffed bell peppers on a baking sheet and bake in the preheated oven for 20-25 minutes until the peppers are tender and the filling is heated through.
6. Remove from the oven and let them cool slightly.
7. Serve the stuffed peppers with optional toppings such as shredded cheese, avocado slices, sour cream, and salsa.

Nutrition information per serving:
- Calories: 252
- Protein: 11g
- Carbohydrates: 47g
- Fat: 3g
- Fiber: 11g

RECIPE 9: GLUTEN-FREE SPINACH AND FETA OMELETTE CUPS

Cooking time: 20 minutes
Servings: 2
Ingredients:
- 4 large eggs
- 1/4 cup milk
- Salt and pepper, to taste
- 1 tablespoon olive oil
- : cherry tomatoes, chopped fresh herbs (such as parsley or chives)
- 1 cup packed fresh spinach, chopped
- 1/4 cup crumbled feta cheese
- Optional toppings

Instructions:

1. Preheat the oven to 350°F (175°C). Grease a muffin tin or line it with silicone liners.
2. In a bowl, whisk together the eggs, milk, salt, and pepper.
3. Heat the olive oil in a frying pan over medium heat. Add the chopped spinach and cook until wilted, about 2-3 minutes.
4. Divide the cooked spinach evenly among the muffin cups.
5. Pour the egg mixture over the spinach in each cup, filling them about 3/4 full.
6. Sprinkle the crumbled feta cheese on top of each cup.
7. Bake in the preheated oven for 12-15 minutes until the eggs are set and the tops are lightly golden.
8. Remove from the oven and let them cool slightly before removing them from the muffin tin.
9. Serve the omelette cups warm, garnished with cherry tomatoes and fresh herbs if desired.

Nutrition information per serving (3 omelette cups):
- Calories: 202
- Protein: 15g
- Carbohydrates: 3g
- Fat: 14g
- fibre: 1g

RECIPE 10: GLUTEN-FREE THAI PEANUT CHICKEN STIR-FRY

Cooking time: 30 minutes
Servings: 2
Ingredients:

- 2 boneless, skinless chicken breasts, thinly sliced
- 2 tablespoons gluten-free soy sauce
- 1 tablespoon rice vinegar
- 1 tablespoon honey or maple syrup
- 1 tablespoon peanut butter
- 1 tablespoon olive oil
- 1 garlic clove, minced
- 1 red bell pepper, thinly sliced
- 1 medium carrot, thinly sliced
- 1 cup broccoli florets
- Optional
- toppings: chopped peanuts, sliced green onions, lime wedges

Instructions:
1. In a small bowl, whisk together the gluten-free soy sauce, rice vinegar, honey or maple syrup, and peanut butter until well combined. Set aside.
2. Heat the olive oil in a large frying pan or wok over medium-high heat.
3. Add the minced garlic to the pan and sauté for 1 minute until fragrant.
4. Add the sliced chicken to the pan and stir-fry until cooked through, about 5-6 minutes.
5. Add the sliced bell pepper, carrot, and broccoli florets to the pan. Stir-fry for an additional 3-4 minutes until the vegetables are tender-crisp.
6. Pour the prepared sauce over the chicken and vegetables. Stir well to coat everything evenly. Cook for 1-2 minutes until the sauce thickens slightly.
7. Remove from heat and garnish with chopped peanuts, sliced green onions, and lime wedges if desired.
8. Serve the Thai peanut chicken stir-fry over cooked rice or noodles, if desired.

Nutrition information per serving (excluding rice/noodles):

- Calories: 296
- Protein: 28g
- Carbohydrates: 19g
- Fat: 11g
- fibre: 4g

RECIPE 11: GLUTEN-FREE BLUEBERRY MUFFINS

Cooking time: 25 minutes
Servings: 12 muffins
Ingredients:

- 2 cups gluten-free all-purpose flour blend
- 1/2 cup granulated sugar
- 2 teaspoons baking powder
- 1/2 teaspoon baking soda
- 1/2 teaspoon salt
- frozen blueberries
- 1 cup unsweetened almond milk (or any milk of your choice)
- 1/4 cup melted coconut oil (or vegetable oil)
- 2 large eggs
- 1 teaspoon vanilla extract
- 1 cup fresh or

Instructions:
1. Preheat the oven to 375°F (190°C). Line a muffin tin with paper liners or grease it lightly.

2. In a large bowl, whisk together the gluten-free flour blend, sugar, baking powder, baking soda, and salt.
3. In a separate bowl, whisk together the almond milk, melted coconut oil, eggs, and vanilla extract.
4. Pour the wet ingredients into the dry ingredients and stir until just combined. Be careful not to over mix.
5. Gently fold in the blueberries.
6. Divide the batter evenly among the muffin cups, filling each about 2/3 full.
7. Bake in the preheated oven for 18-22 minutes, or until a toothpick inserted into the centre of a muffin comes out clean.
8. Allow the muffins to cool in the tin for a few minutes, then transfer them to a wire rack to cool completely.
9. Enjoy the blueberry muffins as a delicious gluten-free breakfast treat!

Nutrition information per serving (1 muffin):
- Calories: 187
- Protein: 3g
- Carbohydrates: 27g
- Fat: 8g
- fibre: 1g

RECIPE 12: GLUTEN-FREE QUINOA SALAD WITH LEMON-HERB DRESSING

Preparation time: 30 minutes
Servings: 4
Ingredients:
- 1 cup quinoa
- 2 cups water or vegetable broth
- 1 cucumber, diced
- 1 red bell pepper, diced
- 1/4 cup red onion, finely chopped
- , to taste
- 1/4 cup chopped fresh parsley
- 1/4 cup chopped fresh mint
- Juice of 1 lemon
- 3 tablespoons olive oil
- Salt and pepper

Instructions:
1. Rinse the quinoa thoroughly under cold water.
2. In a saucepan, combine the quinoa and water or vegetable broth. Bring to a boil, then reduce the heat to low, cover, and simmer for 15-20 minutes or until the liquid is absorbed and the quinoa is tender.
3. Remove the cooked quinoa from the heat and let it cool.
4. In a large bowl, combine the cooked quinoa, diced cucumber, diced red bell pepper, chopped red onion, parsley, and mint.
5. In a small bowl, whisk together the lemon juice, olive oil, salt, and pepper to make the dressing.
6. Pour the dressing over the quinoa salad and toss well to coat all the ingredients.
7. Adjust the seasoning if needed.
8. Let the salad sit for about 10 minutes to allow the flavours to meld.
9. Serve the quinoa salad as a refreshing gluten-free side dish or light lunch.

Nutrition information per serving:
- Calories: 265
- Protein: 6g
- Carbohydrates: 35g

- Fat: 12g
- fibre: 5g

RECIPE 13: GLUTEN-FREE BANANA BREAD

Cooking time: 1 hour
Servings: 8
Ingredients:
- 3 ripe bananas, mashed
- 1/4 cup melted coconut oil (or vegetable oil)
- 1/4 cup honey or maple syrup
- 2 large eggs
- 1 teaspoon vanilla extract
- 1 3/4 cups gluten-free all-purpose flour blend
- 1 teaspoon baking soda
- 1/2 teaspoon salt
- Optional add-ins: chopped nuts, chocolate chips, dried fruit

Instructions:
1. Preheat the oven to 350°F (175°C). Grease a loaf pan and set aside.
2. In a large bowl, whisk together the mashed bananas, melted coconut oil, honey or maple syrup, eggs, and vanilla extract until well combined.
3. In a separate bowl, whisk together the gluten-free all-purpose flour, baking soda, and salt.
4. Gradually add the dry ingredients to the wet ingredients, stirring until just combined. Be careful not to over mix.
5. If desired, fold in any optional add-ins like chopped nuts, chocolate chips, or dried fruit.
6. Pour the batter into the greased loaf pan and spread it evenly.
7. Bake in the preheated oven for 50-60 minutes, or until a toothpick inserted into the center of the bread comes out clean.
8. Allow the banana bread to cool in the pan for about 10 minutes, then transfer it to a wire rack to cool completely.
9. Slice and serve the gluten-free banana bread as a delicious breakfast or snack option.

Nutrition information per serving (1 slice):
- Calories: 256
- Protein: 4g
- Carbohydrates: 43g
- Fat: 9g
- fibre: 3g

RECIPE 14: GLUTEN-FREE QUINOA FRIED RICE

Cooking time: 30 minutes
Servings: 4
Ingredients:
- 1 cup quinoa
- 2 cups water
- 2 tablespoons gluten-free soy sauce
- 1 tablespoon sesame oil
- 1 tablespoon olive oil
- 2 cloves garlic, minced
- 1 cup mixed vegetables (such as diced carrots, peas, and corn)
- 2 large eggs, lightly beaten
- 2 green onions, chopped
- Salt and pepper, to taste

Instructions:
1. Rinse the quinoa thoroughly under cold water.
2. In a saucepan, combine the quinoa and water. Bring to a boil, then reduce the heat to low, cover, and simmer for 15-20 minutes or until the water is absorbed and the quinoa is tender.
3. Remove the cooked quinoa from the heat and let it cool.
4. In a small bowl, whisk together the gluten-free soy sauce and sesame oil. Set aside.

5. Heat the olive oil in a large frying pan or wok over medium-high heat.
6. Add the minced garlic to the pan and sauté for 1 minute until fragrant.
7. Add the mixed vegetables to the pan and stir-fry for about 5 minutes until tender.
8. Push the vegetables to one side of the pan and pour the beaten eggs onto the other side. Scramble the eggs until cooked through.
9. Add the cooked quinoa to the pan and pour the soy sauce mixture over it. Stir well to combine all the ingredients and coat the quinoa evenly.
10. Cook for an additional 2-3 minutes until everything is heated through.
11. Stir in the chopped green onions and season with salt and pepper to taste.
12. Serve the gluten-free quinoa fried rice as a nutritious and satisfying meal.

Nutrition information per serving:
- Calories: 249
- Protein: 9g
- Carbohydrates: 38g
- Fat: 7g
- Fiber: 4g

RECIPE 15: GLUTEN-FREE OVERNIGHT OATS

Preparation time: 5 minutes (plus overnight soaking)
Servings: 1
Ingredients:
- 1/2 cup gluten-free rolled oats
- 1/2 cup unsweetened almond milk (or any milk of your choice)
- 1 tablespoon chia seeds
- berries, sliced banana, chopped nuts, shredded coconut
- 1 tablespoon honey or maple syrup
- 1/4 teaspoon vanilla extract
- Toppings: fresh

Instructions:
1. In a jar or container with a lid, combine the rolled oats, almond milk, chia seeds, honey or maple syrup, and vanilla extract.
2. Stir well to ensure all the ingredients are fully combined.
3. Cover the jar or container and refrigerate overnight or for at least 4 hours to allow the oats and chia seeds to soften and absorb the liquid.
4. In the morning, give the mixture a good stir and add your desired toppings, such as fresh berries, sliced banana, chopped nuts, or shredded coconut.
5. Enjoy the gluten-free overnight oats as a convenient and nutritious breakfast option.

Nutrition information per serving:
- Calories: 288
- Protein: 8g
- Carbohydrates: 46g
- Fat: 9g
- Fiber: 9g

RECIPE 16: GLUTEN-FREE CHICKEN AND VEGETABLE STIR-FRY

Cooking time: 30 minutes
Servings: 2
Ingredients:
- 2 boneless, skinless chicken breasts, sliced into thin strips
- 2 tablespoons gluten-free soy sauce
- 1 tablespoon rice vinegar
- 1 tablespoon honey or maple syrup
- 1 tablespoon olive oil
- 2 cloves garlic, minced
- 1 teaspoon grated fresh ginger
- 1 red bell pepper, sliced
- 1 small zucchini, sliced

- 1 cup broccoli florets
- Salt and pepper, to taste
- sliced green onions, sesame seeds
- Optional garnish:

Instructions:
1. In a small bowl, whisk together the gluten-free soy sauce, rice vinegar, honey or maple syrup. Set aside.
2. Heat the olive oil in a large frying pan or wok over medium-high heat.
3. Add the minced garlic and grated ginger to the pan and cook for 1 minute until fragrant.
4. Add the sliced chicken to the pan and stir-fry until cooked through, about 5-6 minutes.
5. Add the sliced bell pepper, zucchini, and broccoli florets to the pan. Stir-fry for an additional 3-4 minutes until the vegetables are tender-crisp.
6. Pour the soy sauce mixture over the chicken and vegetables. Stir well to coat everything evenly. Cook for 1-2 minutes until the sauce thickens slightly.
7. Season with salt and pepper to taste.
8. Remove from heat and garnish with sliced green onions and sesame seeds if desired.
9. Serve the gluten-free chicken and vegetable stir-fry over cooked rice or noodles, if desired.

Nutrition information per serving (excluding rice/noodles):
- Calories: 252
- Protein: 28g
- Carbohydrates: 16g
- Fat: 7g
- Fiber: 3g

RECIPE 17: GLUTEN-FREE ZUCCHINI FRITTERS

Preparation time: 15 minutes
Cooking time: 15 minutes
Servings: 4
Ingredients:
- 2 cups grated zucchini (about 2 medium-sized zucchini)
- 1/2 teaspoon salt
- 1/4 cup grated Parmesan cheese
- 1/4 cup gluten-free breadcrumbs
- 2 green onions, finely chopped
- 2 cloves garlic, minced
- 2 large eggs, lightly beaten
- 2 tablespoons chopped fresh herbs (such as parsley or dill)
- 2 tablespoons olive oil

Instructions:
1. Place the grated zucchini in a colander and sprinkle with salt. Let it sit for 10 minutes to allow excess moisture to drain.
2. Squeeze the grated zucchini to remove any remaining moisture.
3. In a large bowl, combine the grated zucchini, Parmesan cheese, breadcrumbs, green onions, garlic, beaten eggs, and chopped herbs. Mix well to combine all the ingredients.
4. Heat the olive oil in a large frying pan over medium heat.
5. Using a spoon or your hands, scoop about 2 tablespoons of the zucchini mixture and shape it into a fritter. Place it in the frying pan and flatten it slightly with a spatula. Repeat with the remaining mixture, leaving some space between each fritter.
6. Cook the fritters for about 3-4 minutes per side, or until golden brown and crispy.
7. Transfer the cooked fritters to a paper towel-lined plate to absorb any excess oil.
8. Serve the gluten-free zucchini fritters as a delicious appetizer, side dish, or light meal.

Nutrition information per serving (4 fritters):

- Calories: 132
- Protein: 6g
- Carbohydrates: 9g
- Fat: 8g and Fibres: 2g

RECIPE 18: GLUTEN-FREE CHICKEN AND VEGETABLE CURRY

Cooking time: 30 minutes
Servings: 4
Ingredients:
- 2 tablespoons olive oil
- 1 onion, diced
- 2 cloves garlic, minced
- 1 tablespoon grated fresh ginger
- 2 tablespoons gluten-free curry powder
- 1 teaspoon ground turmeric
- 1 teaspoon ground cumin
- 1 teaspoon ground coriander
- 1/2 teaspoon red pepper flakes (adjust to taste)
- or gluten-free naan, for serving
- 1 can (14 oz) coconut milk
- 1 cup chicken broth
- 2 boneless, skinless chicken breasts, cut into bite-sized pieces
- 2 cups mixed vegetables (such as bell peppers, carrots, and peas)
- Salt and pepper, to taste
- Fresh cilantro, for garnish
- Cooked rice

Instructions:
1. Heat the olive oil in a large pot or skillet over medium heat.
2. Add the diced onion to the pot and sauté for about 5 minutes until softened.
3. Add the minced garlic and grated ginger to the pot and sauté for an additional 1 minute until fragrant.
4. Stir in the curry powder, turmeric, cumin, coriander, and red pepper flakes. Cook for about 1 minute until the spices are aromatic.
5. Pour in the coconut milk and chicken broth. Stir well to combine.
6. Add the chicken pieces to the pot and simmer for about 10 minutes until cooked through.
7. Add the mixed vegetables to the pot and cook for an additional 5 minutes until the vegetables are tender.
8. Season with salt and pepper to taste.
9. Serve the gluten-free chicken and vegetable curry over cooked rice or with gluten-free naan bread.
10. Garnish with fresh cilantro before serving.

Nutrition information per serving (excluding rice/naan):
- Calories: 323
- Protein: 23g
- Carbohydrates: 14g
- Fat: 21g
- fibre: 3g

RECIPE 19: GLUTEN-FREE CHOCOLATE CHIA PUDDING

Preparation time: 10 minutes (plus chilling time)
Servings: 2
Ingredients:
1. 1 cup unsweetened almond milk (or any milk of your choice)
2. 1/4 cup chia seeds
3. 2 tablespoons unsweetened cocoa powder
4. 2 tablespoons honey or maple syrup
5. 1/2 teaspoon vanilla extract

6. Optional toppings: sliced bananas, berries, shredded coconut, chopped nuts

Instructions:
1. In a bowl, whisk together the almond milk, chia seeds, cocoa powder, honey or maple syrup, and vanilla extract until well combined.
2. Let the mixture sit for 5 minutes, then whisk again to prevent clumping.
3. Cover the bowl and refrigerate for at least 2 hours or overnight until the mixture thickens and becomes pudding-like in consistency.
4. Before serving, give the chia pudding a good stir.
5. Divide the pudding into serving bowls or glasses.
6. Top each portion with sliced bananas, berries, shredded coconut, and chopped nuts, if desired.
7. Enjoy the chocolate chia pudding as a delightful gluten-free breakfast or dessert option.

Nutrition information per serving (without toppings):
- Calories: 173
- Protein: 6g
- Carbohydrates: 22g
- Fat: 8g
- fibre: 11g

RECIPE 20: GLUTEN-FREE SHRIMP STIR-FRY WITH VEGETABLES

Cooking time: 30 minutes
Servings: 2
Ingredients:
- 1 tablespoon olive oil
- 8 oz (225g) large shrimp, peeled and deveined
- Salt and pepper, to taste
- 1 red bell pepper, sliced
- 1 small zucchini, sliced
- sliced green onions, sesame seeds
- 1 cup sliced mushrooms
- 2 cloves garlic, minced
- 1 tablespoon gluten-free soy sauce
- 1 tablespoon honey or maple syrup
- 1 teaspoon grated fresh ginger
- Optional garnish:

Instructions:
1. Heat the olive oil in a large frying pan or wok over medium-high heat.
2. Season the shrimp with salt and pepper. Add them to the pan and cook for 2-3 minutes on each side until pink and cooked through. Remove the shrimp from the pan and set aside.
3. In the same pan, add the sliced bell pepper, zucchini, mushrooms, and minced garlic. Stir-fry for about 5 minutes until the vegetables are tender-crisp.
4. In a small bowl, whisk together the gluten-free soy sauce, honey or maple syrup, and grated ginger.
5. Return the cooked shrimp to the pan and pour the sauce over the shrimp and vegetables. Stir well to coat everything evenly.
6. Cook for an additional 2-3 minutes until heated through.
7. Remove from heat and garnish with sliced green onions and sesame seeds if desired.
8. Serve the gluten-free shrimp stir-fry with vegetables over cooked rice or noodles, if desired.

Nutrition information per serving (excluding rice/noodles):
- Calories: 201
- Protein: 22g
- Carbohydrates: 17g
- Fat: 6g
- Fiber: 3g

RECIPE 21: GLUTEN-FREE BANANA PANCAKES

Preparation time: 10 minutes
Cooking time: 10 minutes
Servings: 2-3 (approximately 6 pancakes)
Ingredients:
- 2 ripe bananas
- 2 large eggs
- 1/2 cup gluten-free oat flour
- 1/2 teaspoon baking powder
- 1/2 teaspoon ground cinnamon
- Pinch of salt
- Optional toppings
- : sliced bananas, berries, maple syrup, nuts, or coconut flakes

Instructions:
1. In a mixing bowl, mash the ripe bananas with a fork until smooth.
2. Add the eggs to the mashed bananas and whisk together until well combined.
3. In a separate bowl, whisk together the oat flour, baking powder, ground cinnamon, and salt.
4. Add the dry ingredients to the banana mixture and stir until just combined. Do not overmix.
5. Heat a non-stick skillet or griddle over medium heat and lightly grease it with cooking spray or oil.
6. Pour about 1/4 cup of the pancake batter onto the hot skillet for each pancake.
7. Cook for 2-3 minutes until bubbles start to form on the surface, then flip the pancake and cook for an additional 1-2 minutes on the other side until golden brown.
8. Repeat with the remaining batter.
9. Serve the gluten-free banana pancakes warm with your favorite toppings, such as sliced bananas, berries, maple syrup, nuts, or coconut flakes.

Nutrition information per serving (3 pancakes):
- C
- calories: 214
- Protein: 8g
- Carbohydrates: 40g
- Fat: 4g
- fibre: 6g

RECIPE 22: GLUTEN-FREE CHICKEN STIR-FRY WITH BROCCOLI AND CASHEWS

Cooking time: 30 minutes
Servings: 2
Ingredients:
- 2 boneless, skinless chicken breasts cut into bite-sized pieces
- 2 tablespoons gluten-free soy sauce
- 2 tablespoons rice vinegar
- 1 tablespoon honey or maple syrup
- 1 tablespoon sesame oil
- 1 tablespoon olive oil
- : sliced green onions, sesame seeds
- 2 cloves garlic, minced
- 1 teaspoon grated fresh ginger
- 2 cups broccoli florets
- 1/2 cup unsalted cashews
- Salt and pepper, to taste
- Optional garnish

Instructions:
1. In a small bowl, whisk together the gluten-free soy sauce, rice vinegar, honey or maple syrup, and sesame oil. Set aside.
2. Heat the olive oil in a large frying pan or wok over medium-high heat.

3. Add the minced garlic and grated ginger to the pan and cook for 1 minute until fragrant.
4. Add the chicken pieces to the pan and stir-fry until cooked through, about 5-6 minutes.
5. Add the broccoli florets and cashews to the pan and stir-fry for an additional 3-4 minutes until the broccoli is tender-crisp.
6. Pour the sauce over the chicken, broccoli, and cashews. Stir well to coat everything evenly. Cook for 1-2 minutes until the sauce thickens slightly.
7. Season with salt and pepper to taste.
8. Remove from heat and garnish with sliced green onions and sesame seeds if desired.
9. Serve the gluten-free chicken stir-fry with broccoli and cashews over cooked rice or quinoa, if desired.

Nutrition information per serving (excluding rice/quinoa):
- Calories: 373
- Protein: 31g
- Carbohydrates: 20g
- Fat: 19g
- fibre: 4g

Gluten-Free Lunch Recipes

Recipe 1: Quinoa Salad with Roasted Vegetables
Cooking Time: 30 minutes
Serves: 2
Ingredients:
- 1 cup quinoa
- 2 cups water
- 1 small red bell pepper, sliced
- 1 small yellow bell pepper, sliced
- 1 small zucchini, sliced
- 1 small red onion, sliced
- 2 tablespoons olive oil
- Salt and pepper to taste
- Fresh parsley, chopped, for garnish

Instructions:
1. Preheat the oven to 200°C (400°F).
2. Rinse the quinoa under cold water and drain.
3. In a saucepan, bring the water to a boil. Add the quinoa and simmer for 15 minutes or until cooked.
4. Meanwhile, place the sliced bell peppers, zucchini, and red onion on a baking sheet. Drizzle with olive oil and season with salt and pepper.
5. Roast the vegetables in the preheated oven for 15 minutes or until they are tender and slightly charred.
6. Once the quinoa and vegetables are ready, combine them in a bowl. Toss gently to mix.
7. Garnish with fresh parsley and serve warm or at room temperature.

Nutrition Information (per serving):
- Calories: 320
- Protein: 8g
- Carbohydrates: 50g
- Fat: 12g
- fibre: 6g

Recipe 2: Thai Chicken Lettuce Wraps
Cooking Time: 30 minutes
Serves: 2
Ingredients:
- 2 boneless, skinless chicken breasts, diced
- 2 tablespoons gluten-free soy sauce
- 1 tablespoon fish sauce
- 1 tablespoon lime juice
- 1 tablespoon honey
- 1 tablespoon vegetable oil
- 1 garlic clove, minced
- 1 red chilli, finely chopped
- 1/4 cup fresh mint leaves, chopped
- 1/4 cup fresh cilantro leaves, chopped
- 8 large lettuce leaves

Instructions:
1. In a small bowl, whisk together the gluten-free soy sauce, fish sauce, lime juice, and honey. Set aside.
2. Heat the vegetable oil in a skillet over medium-high heat. Add the minced garlic and chopped chilli. Sauté for 1 minute until fragrant.
3. Add the diced chicken to the skillet and cook until browned and cooked through, about 6-8 minutes.
4. Pour the prepared sauce over the cooked chicken and stir well to coat.
5. Remove the skillet from heat and add the chopped mint and cilantro leaves. Toss to combine.

6. Spoon the chicken mixture onto the lettuce leaves, dividing it equally among them.
7. Roll up the lettuce leaves to create wraps and secure them with toothpicks if needed.
8. Serve the Thai chicken lettuce wraps as a light and refreshing lunch option.

Nutrition Information (per serving):
- Calories: 280
- Protein: 28g
- Carbohydrates: 16g
- Fat: 12g
- fibre: 4g

RECIPE 3: SMASHED AVOCADO CHICKPEA SALAD SANDWICH

Cooking Time: 30 minutes
Serves: 2
Ingredients:
- 1 cans (400g) chickpeas, drained and rinsed
- 1 ripe avocado
- 2 tablespoons fresh lemon juice
- 2 tablespoons chopped fresh cilantro
- and sliced tomatoes for serving
- 1/4 teaspoon garlic powder
- Salt and pepper to taste
- 4 slices gluten-free bread
- Lettuce leaves

Instructions:
1. In a bowl, add the chickpeas and mash them lightly with a fork or potato masher.
2. In a separate bowl, mash the ripe avocado with a fork until creamy.
3. Add the mashed avocado, lemon juice, chopped cilantro, garlic powder, salt, and pepper to the bowl with mashed chickpeas. Stir well to combine all the ingredients.
4. Toast the gluten-free bread slices to your liking.
5. Spread the smashed avocado chickpea mixture evenly onto two slices of bread.
6. Top with lettuce leaves and sliced tomatoes, then cover with the remaining bread slices.
7. Cut the sandwiches in half and serve as a delicious gluten-free lunch option.

Nutrition Information (per serving):
- Calories: 380
- Protein: 14g
- Carbohydrates: 52g
- Fat: 14g
- fibre: 14g

RECIPE 4: SPINACH AND FETA STUFFED CHICKEN BREAST

Cooking Time: 30 minutes
Serves: 2
Ingredients:
- 2 boneless, skinless chicken breasts
- 2 cups fresh spinach leaves
- 1/4 cup crumbled feta cheese
- 1 tablespoon olive oil
- Salt and pepper to taste

Instructions:
1. Preheat the oven to 200°C (400°F).
2. Butterfly the chicken breasts by slicing them horizontally but not all the way through, creating a pocket.
3. Stuff each chicken breast with spinach leaves and crumbled feta cheese.
4. Season the chicken breasts with salt and pepper.
5. Heat the olive oil in an oven-safe skillet over medium-high heat.
6. Place the stuffed chicken breasts in the skillet and cook for 3-4 minutes on each side until browned.

7. Transfer the skillet to the preheated oven and bake for 15-20 minutes or until the chicken is cooked through.
8. Serve the spinach and feta stuffed chicken breasts with a side salad or steamed vegetables.

Nutrition Information (per serving):
- Calories: 320
- Protein: 40g
- Carbohydrates: 2g
- Fat: 16g
- fibre: 1g

RECIPE 5: CAULIFLOWER FRIED RICE

Cooking Time: 30 minutes
Serves: 2
Ingredients:
- 1 small head of cauliflower, grated or finely chopped
- 1 tablespoon vegetable oil
- 2 garlic cloves, minced
- 1 small onion, diced
- 1 medium carrot, diced
- 1/2 cup frozen peas
- 2 tablespoons gluten-free soy sauce
- 2 eggs, beaten
- Salt and pepper to taste
- Chopped green onions for garnish

Instructions:
1. Heat the vegetable oil in a large skillet or wok over medium heat.
2. Add the minced garlic, diced onion, and diced carrot. Sauté for 3-4 minutes until the vegetables are slightly softened.
3. Add the grated cauliflower to the skillet and cook for an additional 4-5 minutes, stirring occasionally.
4. Push the cauliflower mixture to one side of the skillet and pour the beaten eggs onto the other side. Scramble the eggs until cooked.
5. Mix the scrambled eggs with the cauliflower mixture.
6. Add the frozen peas and gluten-free soy sauce to the skillet. Stir well to combine all the ingredients.
7. Season with salt and pepper to taste.
8. Cook for another 3-4 minutes until the peas are heated through.
9. Garnish with chopped green onions and serve the cauliflower fried rice as a delicious gluten-free lunch option.

Nutrition Information (per serving):
- Calories: 220
- Protein: 11g
- Carbohydrates: 20g
- Fat: 11g
- fibre: 8g

RECIPE 6: CAPRESE QUINOA STUFFED PEPPERS

Cooking Time: 30 minutes
Serves: 2
Ingredients:
- 2 large bell peppers (any colour), halved and seeds removed
- 1 cup cooked quinoa
- 1 cup cherry tomatoes, halved
- to taste
- 1/2 cup fresh mozzarella cheese, diced
- 2 tablespoons chopped fresh basil
- 1 tablespoon balsamic glaze
- Salt and pepper

Instructions:
1. Preheat the oven to 200°C (400°F).
2. Place the bell pepper halves on a baking sheet, cut side up.
3. In a bowl, combine the cooked quinoa, cherry tomatoes, fresh mozzarella, chopped basil, balsamic glaze, salt, and pepper. Stir well to mix all the ingredients.
4. Spoon the quinoa mixture evenly into each bell pepper half, pressing it down gently.
5. Bake in the preheated oven for 15-20 minutes or until the bell peppers are tender and the filling is heated through.
6. Remove from the oven and let them cool slightly before serving.
7. Enjoy the Caprese quinoa stuffed peppers as a tasty and filling gluten-free lunch option.

Nutrition Information (per serving):
- Calories: 280
- Protein: 12g
- Carbohydrates: 32g
- Fat: 11g
- fibre: 5g

RECIPE 7: TUNA AND AVOCADO LETTUCE WRAPS
Cooking Time: 15 minutes
Serves: 2
Ingredients:
- 1 cans (160g) tuna, drained
- 1 ripe avocado, mashed
- 1 tablespoon lemon juice
- leaves
- 2 tablespoons chopped fresh parsley
- Salt and pepper to taste
- 4 large lettuce

Instructions:
1. In a bowl, combine the drained tuna, mashed avocado, lemon juice, chopped parsley, salt, and pepper. Mix well until all the ingredients are combined.
2. Place a spoonful of the tuna and avocado mixture onto each lettuce leaf.
3. Roll up the lettuce leaves to create wraps.
4. Serve the tuna and avocado lettuce wraps as a light and protein-packed gluten-free lunch option.

Nutrition Information (per serving):
- Calories: 220
- Protein: 20g
- Carbohydrates: 10g
- Fat: 12g
- fibre: 6g

RECIPE 8: GREEK SALAD WITH GRILLED CHICKEN
Cooking Time: 30 minutes
Serves: 2
Ingredients:
- 2 boneless, skinless chicken breasts
- 1 tablespoon olive oil
- 1 teaspoon dried oregano
- Salt and pepper to taste
- 4 cups mixed salad greens
- 1 cup cherry tomatoes, halved
- olive oil
- 1/2 cucumber, sliced
- 1/2 red onion, thinly sliced
- 1/4 cup Kalamata olives, pitted
- 1/4 cup crumbled feta cheese
- Juice of 1 lemon
- 2 tablespoons

Instructions:

1. Preheat a grill or grill pan over medium-high heat.
2. Brush the chicken breasts with olive oil and sprinkle with dried oregano, salt, and pepper.
3. Grill the chicken breasts for about 6-8 minutes per side or until cooked through.
4. Remove the chicken from the grill and let it rest for a few minutes before slicing.
5. In a large bowl, combine the salad greens, cherry tomatoes, cucumber, red onion, Kalamata olives, and crumbled feta cheese.
6. In a small bowl, whisk together the lemon juice and olive oil to make the dressing.
7. Add the grilled chicken slices to the salad and drizzle with the lemon dressing.
8. Toss the salad gently to combine all the ingredients.
9. Serve the Greek salad with grilled chicken as a refreshing and satisfying gluten-free lunch option.

Nutrition Information (per serving):
- Calories: 320
- Protein: 30g
- Carbohydrates: 10g
- 3g
- Fat: 18g
- fibre:

RECIPE 9: ZUCCHINI NOODLES WITH PESTO

Cooking Time: 20 minutes
Serves: 2
Ingredients:
- 2 medium zucchini
- 2 tablespoons olive oil
- 2 cloves garlic, minced
- Salt and pepper to taste
- 1/4 cup homemade or store-bought gluten-free pesto
- Grated Parmesan cheese for garnish (optional)

Instructions:
1. Using a spiralized or a julienne peeler cut the zucchini into noodle-like strips.
2. Heat the olive oil in a large skillet over medium heat.
3. Add the minced garlic to the skillet and sauté for about 1 minute until fragrant.
4. Add the zucchini noodles to the skillet and cook for 3-4 minutes until they are tender but still slightly crisp.
5. Season with salt and pepper to taste.
6. Remove the skillet from heat and add the gluten-free pesto. Toss the zucchini noodles gently to coat them with the pesto sauce.
7. Garnish with grated Parmesan cheese if desired.
8. Serve the zucchini noodles with pesto as a light and flavourful gluten-free lunch option.

Nutrition Information (per serving):
- Calories: 180
- Protein: 5g
- Carbohydrates: 9g
- Fat: 15g
- fibre: 3g

RECIPE 10: QUINOA BLACK BEAN SALAD
Cooking Time: 20 minutes
Serves: 2
Ingredients:
- 1 cup cooked quinoa
- 1 can (400g) black beans, drained and rinsed
- 1 cup cherry tomatoes, halved
- 1/2 cup corn kernels
- 1/4 cup diced red bell pepper
- 1/4 cup diced red onion
- 2 tablespoons chopped fresh cilantro
- Juice of 1 lime
- 2 tablespoons olive oil
- Salt and pepper to taste

Instructions:
1. In a large bowl, combine the cooked quinoa, black beans, cherry tomatoes, corn kernels, diced red bell pepper, diced red onion, and chopped fresh cilantro.
2. In a small bowl, whisk together the lime juice, olive oil, salt, and pepper to make the dressing.
3. Pour the dressing over the quinoa and black bean mixture. Toss well to combine all the ingredients and coat them with the dressing.
4. Adjust the seasoning if needed.
5. Serve the quinoa black bean salad as a nutritious and filling gluten-free lunch option.

Nutrition Information (per serving):
- Calories: 320
- Protein: 12g
- Carbohydrates: 45g
- Fat: 10g
- fibre: 12g

Recipe 11: Baked Salmon with Lemon-Dill Sauce

Cooking Time: 25 minutes
Serves: 2
Ingredients:
- 2 salmon fillets
- 1 tablespoon olive oil
- Salt and pepper to taste
- 1 lemon, thinly sliced
- 1 tablespoon chopped fresh dill
- 1/4 cup Greek yogurt
- Juice of 1/2 lemon

Instructions:
1. Preheat the oven to 200°C (400°F).
2. Brush the salmon fillets with olive oil and season with salt and pepper.
3. Place the salmon fillets on a baking sheet lined with parchment paper.
4. Arrange lemon slices on top of the salmon fillets and sprinkle with chopped fresh dill.
5. Bake in the preheated oven for 15-20 minutes or until the salmon is cooked through.
6. In a small bowl, mix together the Greek yogurt and lemon juice to make the sauce.
7. Serve the baked salmon with the lemon-dill sauce as a protein-rich gluten-free lunch option.

Nutrition Information (per serving):
- Calories: 320
- Protein: 30g
- Carbohydrates: 2g
- Fat: 22g
- fibre: 1g

RECIPE 12: MEXICAN QUINOA STUFFED BELL PEPPERS

Cooking Time: 40 minutes
Serves: 2
Ingredients:
- 2 large bell peppers (any colour), halved and seeds removed
- 1 cup cooked quinoa
- 1 cup black beans, drained and rinsed
- 1 cup corn kernels
- 1/2 cup diced tomatoes
- cheese for topping (optional)
- 1/4 cup diced red onion
- 1/4 cup chopped fresh cilantro
- 1 teaspoon ground cumin
- 1 teaspoon chilli powder
- Salt and pepper to taste
- Grated cheddar

Instructions:
1. Preheat the oven to 180°C (350°F).
2. Place the bell pepper halves on a baking sheet, cut side up.
3. In a large bowl, combine the cooked quinoa, black beans, corn kernels, diced tomatoes, diced red onion, chopped cilantro, ground cumin, chilli powder, salt, and pepper. Mix well.
4. Spoon the quinoa mixture evenly into each bell pepper half.
5. If desired, sprinkle grated cheddar cheese on top of the stuffed peppers.
6. Bake in the preheated oven for 25-30 minutes or until the bell peppers are tender and the filling is heated through.
7. Serve the Mexican quinoa stuffed bell peppers as a flavourful and satisfying gluten-free lunch option.

Nutrition Information (per serving):
- Calories: 320
- Protein: 14g
- Carbohydrates: 56g
- Fat: 4g
- fibre: 12g

RECIPE 13: SHRIMP STIR-FRY WITH VEGETABLES

Cooking Time: 20 minutes
Serves: 2
Ingredients:
- 1 tablespoon vegetable oil
- 1/2 pound shrimp, peeled and deveined
- 1 small onion, thinly sliced
- 1 bell pepper, thinly sliced
- 1 zucchini, thinly sliced
- 1 carrot, julienned
- 1 cup broccoli florets
- onions for garnish
- 2 cloves garlic, minced
- 2 tablespoons gluten-free soy sauce
- 1 tablespoon rice vinegar
- 1 teaspoon honey (or your preferred sweetener)
- Salt and pepper to taste
- Chopped green

Instructions:
1. Heat the vegetable oil in a large skillet or wok over medium-high heat.
2. Add the shrimp to the skillet and cook for 2-3 minutes until they turn pink and opaque. Remove the shrimp from the skillet and set aside.
3. In the same skillet, add the sliced onion, bell pepper, zucchini, carrot, broccoli florets, and minced garlic. Stir-fry for about 4-5 minutes until the vegetables are crisp-tender.

4. In a small bowl, whisk together the gluten-free soy sauce, rice vinegar, honey, salt, and pepper to make the sauce.
5. Return the cooked shrimp to the skillet and pour the sauce over the stir-fried vegetables and shrimp. Stir well to coat everything with the sauce.
6. Cook for an additional 1-2 minutes until everything is heated through.
7. Garnish with chopped green onions and serve the shrimp stir-fry with vegetables as a delicious and protein-packed gluten-free lunch option.

Nutrition Information (per serving):
- Calories: 240
- Protein: 22g
- Carbohydrates: 20g
- Fat: 9g
- fibre: 5g

RECIPE 14: QUINOA SPINACH STUFFED MUSHROOMS
Cooking Time: 30 minutes
Serves: 2
Ingredients:
- 4 large Portobello mushrooms, stems removed
- 1 cup cooked quinoa
- 1 cup chopped spinach
- 1/4 cup diced red bell pepper
- pepper to taste
- 1/4 cup diced red onion
- 2 cloves garlic, minced
- 2 tablespoons grated Parmesan cheese
- 2 tablespoons olive oil
- Salt and

Instructions:
1. Preheat the oven to 200°C (400°F).
2. Place the Portobello mushrooms on a baking sheet, gill side up.
3. In a large bowl, combine the cooked quinoa, chopped spinach, diced red bell pepper, diced red onion, minced garlic, grated Parmesan cheese, olive oil, salt, and pepper. Mix well.
4. Spoon the quinoa mixture into the mushroom caps, pressing it down gently.
5. Bake in the preheated oven for 20 minutes or until the mushrooms are tender and the filling is heated through.
6. Serve the quinoa spinach stuffed mushrooms as a flavourful and nutritious gluten-free lunch option.

Nutrition Information (per serving):
- Calories: 280
- Protein: 12g
- Carbohydrates: 32g
- 8g
- Fat: 12g
- fibre:

RECIPE 15: EGG SALAD LETTUCE WRAPS
Cooking Time: 15 minutes
Serves: 2
Ingredients:
- 4 hard-boiled eggs, peeled and chopped
- 2 tablespoons mayonnaise
- 1 tablespoon Dijon mustard
- 2 tablespoons chopped fresh chives
- Salt and pepper to taste
- 8 large lettuce leaves

Instructions:

1. In a bowl, combine the chopped hard-boiled eggs, mayonnaise, Dijon mustard, chopped fresh chives, salt, and pepper. Mix well to combine all the ingredients.
2. Place a spoonful of the egg salad mixture onto each lettuce leaf.
3. Roll up the lettuce leaves to create wraps.
4. Serve the egg salad lettuce wraps as a light and protein-rich gluten-free lunch option.

Nutrition Information (per serving):
- Calories: 280
- Protein: 16g
- Carbohydrates: 6g
- Fat: 22g
- fibre: 2g

RECIPE 16: MEDITERRANEAN CHICKPEA SALAD
Cooking Time: 15 minutes
Serves: 2
Ingredients:
- 1 cans (400g) chickpeas, drained and rinsed
- 1 cup cherry tomatoes, halved
- 1/2 cucumber, diced
- 1/4 cup diced red onion
- 1/4 cup sliced Kalamata olives
- feta cheese for garnish (optional)
- 2 tablespoons chopped fresh parsley
- Juice of 1 lemon
- 2 tablespoons extra-virgin olive oil
- Salt and pepper to taste
- Crumbled

Instructions:
1. In a large bowl, combine the chickpeas, cherry tomatoes, cucumber, red onion, Kalamata olives, and chopped parsley.
2. In a small bowl, whisk together the lemon juice, olive oil, salt, and pepper to make the dressing.
3. Pour the dressing over the chickpea mixture. Toss well to combine all the ingredients and coat them with the dressing.
4. Adjust the seasoning if needed.
5. Garnish with crumbled feta cheese if desired.
6. Serve the Mediterranean chickpea salad as a refreshing and nutritious gluten-free lunch option.

Nutrition Information (per serving):
- Calories: 320
- Protein: 12g
- Carbohydrates: 44g
- Fat: 12g
- fibre: 12g

RECIPE 17: THAI PEANUT ZUCCHINI NOODLES
Cooking Time: 20 minutes
Serves: 2
Ingredients:
- 2 medium zucchini
- 2 tablespoons peanut butter
- 2 tablespoons gluten-free soy sauce
- 1 tablespoon lime juice
- 1 tablespoon honey (or your preferred sweetener)
- 1 teaspoon sesame oil
- 1/2 teaspoon grated fresh ginger
- 1/4 teaspoon crushed red pepper flakes (optional)
- Chopped

- peanuts and sliced green onions for garnish

Instructions:

1. Using a spiralized or a julienne peeler cut the zucchini into noodle-like strips.
2. In a small bowl, whisk together the peanut butter, gluten-free soy sauce, lime juice, honey, sesame oil, grated ginger, and crushed red pepper flakes (if using) to make the sauce.
3. Heat a large skillet over medium heat and add the zucchini noodles. Cook for about 2-3 minutes until they are slightly softened.
4. Pour the sauce over the zucchini noodles. Stir well to coat the noodles with the sauce and heat through.
5. Remove from heat and garnish with chopped peanuts and sliced green onions.
6. Serve the Thai peanut zucchini noodles as a flavourful and low-carb gluten-free lunch option.

Nutrition Information (per serving):
- Calories: 220
- Protein: 8g
- Carbohydrates: 18g
- Fat: 14g
- fibre: 4g

RECIPE 18: BAKED TURKEY MEATBALLS WITH MARINARA SAUCE

Cooking Time: 25 minutes
Serves: 2
Ingredients:
- 1/2 pound ground turkey
- 1/4 cup gluten-free bread crumbs
- 1/4 cup grated Parmesan cheese
- 1/4 cup chopped fresh parsley
- 1 egg, beaten
- 2 cloves garlic, minced
- for garnish (optional)
- 1/2 teaspoon dried oregano
- 1/2 teaspoon dried basil
- Salt and pepper to taste
- 1 cup marinara sauce (check for gluten-free variety)
- Fresh basil leaves

Instructions:
1. Preheat the oven to 200°C (400°F).
2. In a large bowl, combine the ground turkey, gluten-free bread crumbs, grated Parmesan cheese, chopped fresh parsley, beaten egg, minced garlic, dried oregano, dried basil, salt, and pepper. Mix well to combine all the ingredients.
3. Shape the mixture into small meatballs and place them on a baking sheet lined with parchment paper.
4. Bake in the preheated oven for 20-25 minutes or until the meatballs are cooked through and browned.
5. In a small saucepan, heat the marinara sauce over medium heat until warmed.
6. Place the baked turkey meatballs in a serving dish and pour the marinara sauce over them.
7. Garnish with fresh basil leaves if desired.
8. Serve the baked turkey meatballs with marinara sauce as a protein-packed gluten-free lunch option.

Nutrition Information (per serving):
- Calories: 240
- Protein: 26g
- Carbohydrates: 10g
- Fat: 10g and fibre: 2g

RECIPE 19: QUINOA STUFFED BUTTERNUT SQUASH

Cooking Time: 45 minutes
Serves: 2
Ingredients:

- 1 small butternut squash, halved and seeds removed
- 1 cup cooked quinoa
- 1/2 cup chopped walnuts
- 1/4 cup dried cranberries
- taste
- 1/4 cup crumbled goat cheese
- 2 tablespoons chopped fresh parsley
- 2 tablespoons olive oil
- Salt and pepper to

Instructions:

1. Preheat the oven to 200°C (400°F).
2. Place the butternut squash halves on a baking sheet, cut side up.
3. Drizzle olive oil over the cut sides of the butternut squash and season with salt and pepper.
4. Roast the butternut squash in the preheated oven for 30-35 minutes or until the flesh is tender.
5. Meanwhile, in a bowl, combine the cooked quinoa, chopped walnuts, dried cranberries, crumbled goat cheese, chopped parsley, olive oil, salt, and pepper. Mix well.
6. Remove the roasted butternut squash from the oven and let it cool slightly.
7. Spoon the quinoa mixture into the hollowed-out part of each butternut squash half.
8. Return the stuffed butternut squash halves to the oven and bake for an additional 10 minutes to heat the filling through.
9. Serve the quinoa stuffed butternut squash as a flavourful and hearty gluten-free lunch option.

Nutrition Information (per serving):

- Calories: 420
- Protein: 12g
- Carbohydrates: 50g
- Fat: 22g
- fibre: 8g

RECIPE 20: AVOCADO TUNA SALAD WRAPS

Cooking Time: 10 minutes
Serves: 2
Ingredients:

- 1 cans (160g) tuna, drained
- 1 ripe avocado, mashed
- 2 tablespoons Greek yogurt
- 1 tablespoon lemon juice
- and cucumber for serving
- 2 tablespoons chopped fresh dill
- Salt and pepper to taste
- 4 large lettuce leaves
- Sliced tomatoes

Instructions:

1. In a bowl, combine the drained tuna, mashed avocado, Greek yogurt, lemon juice, chopped fresh dill, salt, and pepper. Mix well to combine all the ingredients.
2. Place a spoonful of the avocado tuna salad onto each lettuce leaf.
3. Top with sliced tomatoes and cucumber.
4. Roll up the lettuce leaves to create wraps.
5. Serve the avocado tuna salad wraps as a creamy and protein-rich gluten-free lunch option.

Nutrition Information (per serving):
- Calories: 320
- Protein: 28g
- Carbohydrates: 16g
- Fat: 18g
- Fiber: 10g

RECIPE 21: CAULIFLOWER FRIED RICE WITH SHRIMP

Cooking Time: 25 minutes
Serves: 2
Ingredients:
- 1 small head of cauliflower, grated or finely chopped
- 1/2 pound shrimp, peeled and deveined
- 2 tablespoons vegetable oil
- 1 small onion, diced
- 1 carrot, diced
- 1/2 cup frozen peas
- 2 cloves garlic, minced
- 2 tablespoons gluten-free soy sauce
- 2 eggs, beaten
- Salt and pepper to taste
- Chopped green onions for garnish

Instructions:
1. Heat 1 tablespoon of vegetable oil in a large skillet or wok over medium heat.
2. Add the shrimp to the skillet and cook for 2-3 minutes until pink and opaque. Remove the shrimp from the skillet and set aside.
3. In the same skillet, add the remaining tablespoon of vegetable oil and sauté the diced onion, carrot, frozen peas, and minced garlic for about 4-5 minutes until the vegetables are tender.
4. Push the vegetables to one side of the skillet and pour the beaten eggs onto the other side. Scramble the eggs until cooked.
5. Mix the scrambled eggs with the vegetables.
6. Add the grated cauliflower to the skillet and cook for an additional 4-5 minutes until it is tender.
7. Add the cooked shrimp back to the skillet.
8. Pour the gluten-free soy sauce over the mixture and stir well to combine all the ingredients.
9. Season with salt and pepper to taste.
10. Cook for another 2-3 minutes until everything is heated through.
11. Garnish with chopped green onions and serve the cauliflower fried rice with shrimp as a flavourful and low-carb gluten-free lunch option.

Nutrition Information (per serving):
- Calories: 280
- Protein: 28g
- Carbohydrates: 16g
- Fat: 10g
- fibre: 6g

RECIPE 22: CAPRESE CHICKEN SALAD

Cooking Time: 20 minutes
Serves: 2
Ingredients:
- 2 boneless, skinless chicken breasts
- 1 tablespoon olive oil
- Salt and pepper to taste
- 1 cup cherry tomatoes, halved
- 1/2 cup fresh mozzarella balls, halved
- 1/4 cup chopped fresh basil
- 2 tablespoons balsamic glaze

Instructions:
- Preheat a grill or grill pan over medium-high heat.
- Brush the chicken breasts with olive oil and season with salt and pepper.

- Grill the chicken breasts for about 6-8 minutes per side or until cooked through.
- Remove the chicken from the grill and let it rest for a few minutes before slicing.
- In a bowl, combine the cherry tomatoes, fresh mozzarella balls, and chopped basil.
- Drizzle the balsamic glaze over the tomato and mozzarella mixture and toss to combine.
- Slice the grilled chicken breasts and arrange them on plates.
- Top the chicken slices with the Caprese tomato and mozzarella mixture.
- Serve the Caprese chicken salad as a light and flavourful gluten-free lunch option.

Nutrition Information (per serving):
- Calories: 280
- Protein: 32g
- Carbohydrates: 8g
- Fat: 14g
- fibre: 1g

RECIPE 23: SWEET POTATO AND BLACK BEAN QUESADILLAS

Cooking Time: 30 minutes
Serves: 2
Ingredients:
- 2 small sweet potatoes, peeled and diced
- 1 tablespoon olive oil
- 1/2 teaspoon ground cumin
- 1/2 teaspoon chilli powder
- Salt and pepper to taste
- , and sour cream for serving (optional)
- 4 gluten-free tortillas
- 1 cup black beans, drained and rinsed
- 1 cup shredded cheddar or Mexican blend cheese
- Salsa, guacamole

Instructions:
1. Preheat the oven to 200°C (400°F).
2. Place the diced sweet potatoes on a baking sheet. Drizzle with olive oil and sprinkle with ground cumin, chilli powder, salt, and pepper. Toss to coat the sweet potatoes evenly.
3. Roast the sweet potatoes in the preheated oven for 20-25 minutes until tender and slightly caramelized.
4. Heat a large skillet over medium heat.
5. Place one tortilla in the skillet and sprinkle half of it with black beans, roasted sweet potatoes, and shredded cheese.
6. Fold the tortilla in half to create a quesadilla and press it gently with a spatula.
7. Cook for about 2-3 minutes per side until the tortilla is crispy and the cheese is melted.
8. Remove the quesadilla from the skillet and repeat the process with the remaining tortilla and ingredients.
9. Cut the quesadillas into wedges and serve with salsa, guacamole, and sour cream if desired.
10. Enjoy the sweet potato and black bean quesadillas as a delicious and filling gluten-free lunch option.

Nutrition Information (per serving):
- Calories: 420
- Protein: 16g
- Carbohydrates: 50g
- Fat: 18g
- fibre: 10g

RECIPE 24: GREEK CHICKEN PITA POCKETS
Cooking Time: 30 minutes
Serves: 2
Ingredients:
- 2 boneless, skinless chicken breasts
- 2 tablespoons Greek yogurt
- 1 tablespoon lemon juice
- 1 teaspoon dried oregano
- Salt and pepper to taste
- 2 gluten-free pita bread rounds
- Tzatziki sauce, chopped tomatoes, cucumbers, and red onions for serving

Instructions:
1. Preheat a grill or grill pan over medium-high heat.
2. In a small bowl, combine the Greek yogurt, lemon juice, dried oregano, salt, and pepper.
3. Brush the chicken breasts with the Greek yogurt mixture, coating them well.
4. Grill the chicken breasts for about 6-8 minutes per side or until cooked through.
5. Remove the chicken from the grill and let it rest for a few minutes before slicing.
6. Cut the gluten-free pita bread rounds in half to create pockets.
7. Stuff each pita pocket with sliced grilled chicken, tzatziki sauce, chopped tomatoes, cucumbers, and red onions.
8. Serve the Greek chicken pita pockets as a flavourful and satisfying gluten-free lunch option.

Nutrition Information (per serving):
- Calories: 320
- Protein: 32g
- Carbohydrates: 22g
- Fat: 10g
- fibre: 4g

RECIPE 25: QUINOA STUFFED AVOCADO BOATS
Cooking Time: 20 minutes
Serves: 2
Ingredients:
- 1 cup cooked quinoa
- 1/2 cup black beans, drained and rinsed
- 1/2 cup corn kernels
- 1/4 cup diced red bell pepper
- 1/4 cup diced red onion
- 2 tablespoons chopped fresh cilantro
- Juice of 1 lime
- 2 ripe avocados, halved and pitted
- Salt and pepper to taste

Instructions:
1. In a bowl, combine the cooked quinoa, black beans, corn kernels, diced red bell pepper, diced red onion, chopped fresh cilantro, lime juice, salt, and pepper. Mix well to combine all the ingredients.
2. Scoop out a small portion of the flesh from each avocado half to create a cavity for the filling.
3. Fill each avocado half with the quinoa mixture, pressing it down gently.
4. Serve the quinoa stuffed avocado boats as a healthy and nutrient-packed gluten-free lunch option.

Nutrition Information (per serving):
- Calories: 340
- Protein: 10g
- Carbohydrates: 32g
- Fat: 22g
- fibre: 14g

Note: Adjust the seasonings and ingredients according to your taste preferences. Enjoy your quick and easy gluten-free lunch!

Gluten-Free Dinner Recipes

Recipe 1: Garlic Lemon Chicken with Roasted Vegetables

Cooking Time: 30 minutes
Serves: 4
Ingredients:

- 4 boneless, skinless chicken breasts
- 2 cloves of garlic, minced
- 1 lemon, juiced and zested
- 2 tablespoons olive oil
- Salt and pepper to taste
- 500g mixed vegetables (carrots, bell peppers, zucchini), chopped
- 1 tablespoon fresh parsley, chopped

Instructions:

1. Preheat the oven to 200°C (180°C fan).
2. In a bowl, combine minced garlic, lemon juice, lemon zest, olive oil, salt, and pepper.
3. Place the chicken breasts in a baking dish and pour the garlic lemon mixture over them. Make sure they are evenly coated.
4. Arrange the chopped vegetables around the chicken breasts.
5. Bake in the preheated oven for 20-25 minutes or until the chicken is cooked through and the vegetables are tender.
6. Sprinkle fresh parsley over the chicken and vegetables before serving.

Nutrition Information per Serving:

- Calories: 350 kcal
- Protein: 30g
- Carbohydrates: 15g
- Fat: 20g
- fibre: 5g

Recipe 2: Shrimp Stir-Fry with Rice Noodles

Cooking Time: 30 minutes
Serves: 2
Ingredients:

- 150g rice noodles
- 250g peeled and deveined shrimp
- 2 tablespoons gluten-free soy sauce
- 1 tablespoon honey
- 1 tablespoon sesame oil
- 1 red bell pepper, thinly sliced
- for garnish
- 1 carrot, julienned
- 1 small onion, thinly sliced
- 2 cloves of garlic, minced
- 1 teaspoon grated ginger
- 2 spring onions, sliced
- Fresh cilantro

Instructions:

1. Cook the rice noodles according to package instructions. Drain and set aside.
2. In a small bowl, whisk together gluten-free soy sauce, honey, and sesame oil.
3. Heat some oil in a wok or large frying pan over medium-high heat. Add the shrimp and stir-fry for 2-3 minutes until pink. Remove from the pan and set aside.
4. In the same pan, add a little more oil and sauté the bell pepper, carrot, onion, garlic, and ginger for 3-4 minutes until the vegetables are tender-crisp.
5. Return the shrimp to the pan and add the cooked rice noodles. Pour the sauce over the ingredients and toss everything together to coat.
6. Cook for an additional 2-3 minutes until heated through.

7. Sprinkle with sliced spring onions and garnish with fresh cilantro before serving.

Nutrition Information per Serving:
- Calories: 420 kcal
- Protein: 25g
- Carbohydrates: 60g
- Fat: 8g
- fibre: 5g

RECIPE 3: QUINOA STUFFED BELL PEPPERS
Cooking Time: 40 minutes
Serves: 4
Ingredients:
- 4 large bell peppers (any colour)
- 1 cup cooked quinoa
- 250g ground beef (or substitute with ground turkey or chicken)
- 1 small onion, chopped
- 2 cloves of garlic, minced
- 1 teaspoon dried oregano
- 1 teaspoon ground cumin
- Salt and pepper to taste
- 200g canned diced tomatoes
- 50g shredded cheddar cheese (optional)
- Fresh parsley for garnish

Instructions:
1. Preheat the oven to 180°C (160°C fan).
2. Cut off the tops of the bell peppers and remove the seeds and membranes. Set them aside.
3. In a frying pan, cook the ground beef over medium heat until browned. Drain any excess fat.
4. Add the chopped onion, minced garlic, dried oregano, ground cumin, salt, and pepper to the pan. Cook for an additional 2-3 minutes until the onion is softened.
5. Stir in the cooked quinoa and diced tomatoes. Cook for another 2-3 minutes until heated through.
6. Stuff the bell peppers with the quinoa and beef mixture, pressing it down lightly. Place the stuffed peppers in a baking dish.
7. Bake in the preheated oven for 25-30 minutes until the peppers are tender.
8. If desired, sprinkle shredded cheddar cheese on top of each pepper during the last 5 minutes of baking.
9. Garnish with fresh parsley before serving.

Nutrition Information per Serving:
- Calories: 350 kcal
- Protein: 20g
- Carbohydrates: 35g
- Fat: 14g
- Fiber: 8g

RECIPE 4: ZUCCHINI NOODLE STIR-FRY WITH CHICKEN
Cooking Time: 25 minutes
Serves: 2
Ingredients:
- 2 medium zucchinis, spiralized into noodles
- 2 chicken breasts, thinly sliced
- 2 tablespoons gluten-free soy sauce
- 1 tablespoon rice vinegar
- 1 tablespoon sesame oil
- 1 tablespoon olive oil
- 1 red bell pepper, thinly sliced
- 1 carrot, julienned
- 2 cloves of garlic, minced
- 1 teaspoon grated ginger
- 2 spring onions, sliced
- Sesame seeds for garnish

Instructions:
1. In a small bowl, whisk together gluten-free soy sauce, rice vinegar, and sesame oil. Set aside.
2. Heat olive oil in a large frying pan or wok over medium-high heat. Add the chicken slices and cook until browned and cooked through. Remove from the pan and set aside.
3. In the same pan, add a little more oil if needed and sauté the bell pepper, carrot, garlic, and ginger for 2-3 minutes until the vegetables are tender-crisp.
4. Add the zucchini noodles to the pan and stir-fry for an additional 2-3 minutes until they are just cooked but still have a slight crunch.
5. Return the cooked chicken to the pan and pour the sauce over the ingredients. Toss everything together to coat.
6. Cook for another minute until heated through.
7. Garnish with sliced spring onions and sprinkle with sesame seeds before serving.

Nutrition Information per Serving:
- Calories: 320 kcal
- Protein: 30g
- Carbohydrates: 12g
- Fat: 16g
- fibre: 4g

RECIPE 5: BAKED SALMON WITH LEMON DILL SAUCE

Cooking Time: 20 minutes
Serves: 2
Ingredients:
- 2 salmon fillets
- 1 lemon, sliced
- 1 tablespoon olive oil
- Salt and pepper to taste
- 2 tablespoons fresh dill, chopped
- 2 tablespoons mayonnaise
- 1 tablespoon Dijon mustard
- 1 tablespoon lemon juice

Instructions:
1. Preheat the oven to 200°C (180°C fan).
2. Place the salmon fillets on a baking sheet lined with parchment paper. Drizzle with olive oil and season with salt and pepper.
3. Arrange lemon slices on top of each salmon fillet.
4. Bake in the preheated oven for 15-18 minutes or until the salmon is cooked through and flakes easily with a fork.
5. In a small bowl, combine fresh dill, mayonnaise, Dijon mustard, and lemon juice. Stir until well combined.
6. Serve the baked salmon with the lemon dill sauce drizzled on top.

Nutrition Information per Serving:
- Calories: 400 kcal
- Protein: 30g
- Carbohydrates: 3g
- Fat: 30g
- fibre: 1g

RECIPE 6: SPINACH AND FETA STUFFED CHICKEN BREAST

Cooking Time: 35 minutes
Serves: 4
Ingredients:
- 4 boneless, skinless chicken breasts
- 100g fresh spinach leaves
- 100g feta cheese, crumbled
- 2 cloves of garlic, minced
- 1 tablespoon olive oil
- Salt and pepper to taste
- 1 lemon, sliced
- Fresh parsley for garnish

Instructions:
1. Preheat the oven to 200°C (180°C fan).
2. Butterfly the chicken breasts by cutting a slit horizontally through the middle, stopping just before the edge, and opening it like a book.
3. In a pan, heat olive oil over medium heat. Add minced garlic and sauté for 1-2 minutes until fragrant.
4. Add fresh spinach leaves to the pan and cook until wilted.
5. Remove the pan from heat and let the spinach cool slightly. Once cooled, stir in the crumbled feta cheese.
6. Stuff each chicken breast with the spinach and feta mixture. Season with salt and pepper.
7. Place the stuffed chicken breasts on a baking sheet lined with parchment paper. Top with lemon slices.
8. Bake in the preheated oven for 25-30 minutes or until the chicken is cooked through and no longer pink in the centre.
9. Garnish with fresh parsley before serving.

Nutrition Information per Serving:
- Calories: 320 kcal
- Protein: 40g
- Carbohydrates: 3g
- Fat: 15g
- Fiber: 1g

RECIPE 7: BEEF AND BROCCOLI STIR-FRY

Cooking Time: 25 minutes
Serves: 4
Ingredients:
- 500g beef sirloin, thinly sliced
- 2 tablespoons gluten-free soy sauce
- 1 tablespoon rice vinegar
- 1 tablespoon honey
- 1 tablespoon corn-starch
- 2 tablespoons olive oil
- 2 cloves of garlic, minced
- 1 teaspoon grated ginger
- 1 broccoli head, cut into florets
- Salt and pepper to taste
- Sesame seeds for garnish

Instructions:
1. In a small bowl, whisk together gluten-free soy sauce, rice vinegar, honey, and cornstarch. Set aside.
2. Heat olive oil in a large frying pan or wok over medium-high heat. Add the beef slices and cook until browned. Remove from the pan and set aside.
3. In the same pan, add a little more oil if needed and sauté the garlic and ginger for 1-2 minutes until fragrant.
4. Add the broccoli florets to the pan and stir-fry for 3-4 minutes until they are bright green and tender-crisp.
5. Return the cooked beef to the pan and pour the sauce over the ingredients. Toss everything together to coat.
6. Cook for another 2-3 minutes until heated through and the sauce has thickened.
7. Season with salt and pepper to taste.
8. Sprinkle with sesame seeds before serving.

Nutrition Information per Serving:
- Calories: 350 kcal
- Protein: 30g
- Carbohydrates: 15g
- Fat: 20g and fibre: 4g

Recipe 8: Spaghetti with Tomato Basil Sauce

Cooking Time: 20 minutes
Serves: 4
Ingredients:

- 300g gluten-free spaghetti
- 2 tablespoons olive oil
- 1 small onion, finely chopped
- 2 cloves of garlic, minced
- 400g canned dice tomatoes
- 2 tablespoons tomato paste
- 1 teaspoon dried oregano
- 1 teaspoon dried basil
- Salt and pepper to taste
- Fresh basil leaves for garnish
- Grated Parmesan cheese (optional)

Instructions:
1. Cook the gluten-free spaghetti according to package instructions. Drain and set aside.
2. In a large saucepan, heat olive oil over medium heat. Add the chopped onion and minced garlic. Sauté until the onion is translucent and fragrant.
3. Add the canned diced tomatoes, tomato paste, dried oregano, dried basil, salt, and pepper to the saucepan. Stir to combine.
4. Simmer the sauce for 10-15 minutes, stirring occasionally, until it has thickened slightly and the flavours have melded together.
5. Add the cooked spaghetti to the saucepan and toss to coat the pasta with the tomato basil sauce.
6. Serve the spaghetti with fresh basil leaves and grated Parmesan cheese, if desired.

Nutrition Information per Serving:

- Calories: 350 kcal
- Protein: 8g
- Carbohydrates: 60g
- Fat: 10g
- fibre: 4g

Recipe 9: Thai Green Curry with Vegetables

Cooking Time: 30 minutes
Serves: 4
Ingredients:

- 1 tablespoon coconut oil
- 1 small onion, sliced
- 2 cloves of garlic, minced
- 1 tablespoon grated ginger
- 2 tablespoons green curry paste (ensure it's gluten-free)
- 400ml can coconut milk
- 200g green beans, trimmed
- 1 red bell pepper, sliced
- 1 courgette, sliced
- 200g baby corn, halved
- 200g tofu, cubed
- Juice of 1 lime
- Fresh coriander for garnish
- Cooked rice, to serve

Instructions:
1. Heat coconut oil in a large saucepan or wok over medium heat. Add the sliced onion, minced garlic, and grated ginger. Sauté for 2-3 minutes until fragrant and the onion is softened.
2. Stir in the green curry paste and cook for another minute.
3. Pour in the coconut milk and bring the mixture to a simmer.
4. Add the green beans, red bell pepper, courgette, and baby corn to the saucepan. Stir to coat the vegetables with the curry sauce.
5. Simmer for 10-15 minutes until the vegetables are tender.
6. Add the cubed tofu and lime juice to the saucepan. Stir gently to combine.
7. Cook for an additional 2-3 minutes until the tofu is heated through.

8. Serve the Thai green curry over cooked rice and garnish with fresh coriander.

Nutrition Information per Serving:
- Calories: 320 kcal
- Protein: 10g
- Carbohydrates: 20g
- Fat: 25g
- Fibre: 5g

RECIPE 10: MEDITERRANEAN QUINOA SALAD
Cooking Time: 20 minutes
Serves: 4
Ingredients:
- 200g quinoa
- 400g canned chickpeas, drained and rinsed
- 200g cherry tomatoes, halved
- 1 cucumber, diced
- 1 red bell pepper, diced
- 1 small red onion, finely chopped
- 100g Kalamata olives, pitted and halved
- 100g feta cheese, crumbled
- Juice of 1 lemon
- 3 tablespoons extra virgin olive oil
- 2 tablespoons fresh parsley, chopped
- Salt and pepper to taste

Instructions:
1. Rinse the quinoa under cold water. Cook the quinoa according to package instructions.
2. In a large bowl, combine the cooked quinoa, chickpeas, cherry tomatoes, cucumber, red bell pepper, red onion, Kalamata olives, and crumbled feta cheese.
3. In a small bowl, whisk together the lemon juice, olive oil, chopped parsley, salt, and pepper.
4. Pour the dressing over the quinoa mixture and toss until well coated.
5. Taste and adjust the seasonings if needed.
6. Serve the Mediterranean quinoa salad at room temperature or chilled.

Nutrition Information per Serving:
- Calories: 400 kcal
- Protein: 15g
- Carbohydrates: 45g
- Fat: 18g
- fibre: 8g

RECIPE 11: EASY CHICKEN AND VEGETABLE STIR-FRY
Cooking Time: 20 minutes
Serves: 2
Ingredients:
- 2 chicken breasts, thinly sliced
- 2 tablespoons gluten-free soy sauce
- 1 tablespoon honey
- 1 tablespoon rice vinegar
- 1 tablespoon sesame oil
- 1 tablespoon olive oil
- 1 red bell pepper, thinly sliced
- 1 carrot, julienned
- 1 small onion, thinly sliced
- 100g sugar snaps peas
- 2 cloves of garlic, minced
- 1 teaspoon grated ginger
- 2 spring onions, sliced
- Sesame seeds for garnish

Instructions:
1. In a small bowl, whisk together gluten-free soy sauce, honey, rice vinegar, and sesame oil. Set aside.
2. Heat olive oil in a large frying pan or wok over medium-high heat. Add the chicken slices and cook until browned and cooked through. Remove from the pan and set aside.

3. In the same pan, add a little more oil if needed and sauté the bell pepper, carrot, onion, sugar snap peas, garlic, and ginger for 3-4 minutes until the vegetables are tender-crisp.
4. Return the cooked chicken to the pan and pour the sauce over the ingredients. Toss everything together to coat.
5. Cook for an additional 2-3 minutes until heated through.
6. Garnish with sliced spring onions and sprinkle with sesame seeds before serving.

Nutrition Information per Serving:
- Calories: 350 kcal
- Protein: 30g
- Carbohydrates: 20g
- Fat: 15g
- Fiber: 5g

RECIPE 12: ZESTY LIME SHRIMP TACOS

Cooking Time: 20 minutes
Serves: 2
Ingredients:
- 200g shrimp, peeled and deveined
- Juice of 2 limes
- 2 tablespoons olive oil
- 1 clove of garlic, minced
- 1 teaspoon chilli powder
- 1/2 teaspoon cumin
- Salt and pepper to taste
- 4 corn tortillas
- 1 avocado, sliced
- Fresh cilantro for garnish

Instructions:
1. In a bowl, combine the lime juice, olive oil, minced garlic, chilli powder, cumin, salt, and pepper.
2. Add the shrimp to the bowl and toss to coat them in the marinade. Let it marinate for 10 minutes.
3. Heat a frying pan over medium heat. Cook the shrimp for 2-3 minutes on each side until pink and cooked through.
4. Warm the corn tortillas in a dry pan or in the oven.
5. Assemble the tacos by placing the cooked shrimp on each tortilla. Top with sliced avocado and garnish with fresh cilantro.
6. Serve the zesty lime shrimp tacos immediately.

Nutrition Information per Serving:
- Calories: 320 kcal
- Protein: 20g
- Carbohydrates: 20g
- Fat: 18g
- fibre: 6g

RECIPE 13: CAPRESE CHICKEN SKILLET

Cooking Time: 20 minutes
Serves: 2
Ingredients:
- 2 boneless, skinless chicken breasts
- Salt and pepper to taste
- 1 tablespoon olive oil
- 2 cloves of garlic, minced
- 200g cherry tomatoes, halved
- 100g fresh mozzarella cheese, sliced
- Fresh basil leaves for garnish
- Balsamic glaze for drizzling (optional)

Instructions:
1. Season the chicken breasts with salt and pepper.
2. Heat olive oil in a skillet over medium heat. Add the chicken breasts and cook for about 6-7 minutes per side, or until cooked through.

3. Remove the chicken from the skillet and set aside.
4. In the same skillet, add minced garlic and cherry tomatoes. Sauté for 2-3 minutes until the tomatoes start to soften.
5. Return the chicken to the skillet and top each breast with slices of fresh mozzarella cheese.
6. Cover the skillet and let it cook for an additional 1-2 minutes until the cheese has melted.
7. Garnish with fresh basil leaves and drizzle with balsamic glaze, if desired.
8. Serve the Caprese chicken skillet with a side salad or cooked vegetables.

Nutrition Information per Serving:
- Calories: 350 kcal
- Protein: 40g
- Carbohydrates: 5g
- Fat: 18g
- fibre: 1g

RECIPE 14: QUINOA STUFFED BELL PEPPERS
Cooking Time: 40 minutes
Serves: 4
Ingredients:
- 4 large bell peppers (any colour)
- 200g quinoa
- 400g canned black beans, drained and rinsed
- 200g canned dice tomatoes
- 1 small onion, finely chopped
- 2 cloves of garlic, minced
- 1 teaspoon cumin
- 1 teaspoon paprika
- Salt and pepper to taste
- Fresh parsley for garnish

Instructions:
1. Preheat the oven to 180°C (160°C fan).
2. Cut off the tops of the bell peppers and remove the seeds and membranes. Set them aside.
3. In a saucepan, cook the quinoa according to package instructions.
4. In a separate pan, sauté the onion and garlic until softened. Add the canned diced tomatoes, black beans, cumin, paprika, salt, and pepper. Cook for a few minutes to heat through.
5. Combine the cooked quinoa with the bean and tomato mixture.
6. Stuff each bell pepper with the quinoa and bean filling.
7. Place the stuffed peppers in a baking dish and cover with foil.
8. Bake in the preheated oven for 30 minutes. Remove the foil and bake for an additional 5-10 minutes until the peppers are tender.
9. Garnish with fresh parsley before serving.

Nutrition Information per Serving:
- Calories: 300 kcal
- Protein: 12g
- Carbohydrates: 55g
- Fat: 4g
- fibre: 12g

RECIPE 15: SALMON AND ASPARAGUS FOIL PACKETS
Cooking Time: 25 minutes
Serves: 2
Ingredients:
- 2 salmon fillets
- 200g asparagus spears, trimmed
- 2 tablespoons olive oil
- 2 cloves of garlic, minced
- 1 lemon, sliced
- Salt and pepper to taste
- Fresh dill for garnish

Instructions:

1. Preheat the oven to 200°C (180°C fan).
2. Cut two large pieces of foil. Place one salmon fillet on each piece of foil.
3. Divide the asparagus spears evenly and place them next to the salmon fillets.
4. Drizzle olive oil over the salmon and asparagus. Sprinkle minced garlic on top. Season with salt and pepper.
5. Place lemon slices on top of each salmon fillet.
6. Fold the sides of the foil over the salmon and asparagus to create a packet. Make sure it is well sealed.
7. Place the foil packets on a baking sheet and bake in the preheated oven for 20 minutes or until the salmon is cooked through and flakes easily with a fork.
8. Carefully open the foil packets, garnish with fresh dill, and serve.

Nutrition Information per Serving:
- Calories: 400 kcal
- Protein: 35g
- Carbohydrates: 8g
- Fat: 25g
- Fiber: 4g

RECIPE 16: TERIYAKI BEEF STIR-FRY

Cooking Time: 20 minutes
Serves: 4
Ingredients:
- 500g beef sirloin, thinly sliced
- 3 tablespoons gluten-free soy sauce
- 2 tablespoons honey
- 2 tablespoons rice vinegar
- 1 tablespoon corn-starch
- 1 tablespoon olive oil
- 1 red bell pepper, thinly sliced
- 1 yellow bell pepper, thinly sliced
- 1 small onion, thinly sliced
- 2 cloves of garlic, minced
- 1 teaspoon grated ginger
- 2 spring onions, sliced
- Sesame seeds for garnish

Instructions:
1. In a small bowl, whisk together gluten-free soy sauce, honey, rice vinegar, and cornstarch. Set aside.
2. Heat olive oil in a large frying pan or wok over medium-high heat. Add the beef slices and cook until browned. Remove from the pan and set aside.
3. In the same pan, add a little more oil if needed and sauté the bell peppers, onion, garlic, and ginger for 2-3 minutes until the vegetables are tender-crisp.
4. Return the cooked beef to the pan and pour the sauce over the ingredients. Toss everything together to coat.
5. Cook for another 2-3 minutes until heated through and the sauce have thickened.
6. Garnish with sliced spring onions and sprinkle with sesame seeds before serving.
7. Serve the teriyaki beef stir-fry over cooked rice or noodles.

Nutrition Information per Serving:
- Calories: 350 kcal
- Protein: 30g
- Carbohydrates: 20g
- Fat: 15g
- fibre: 4g

RECIPE 17: TOMATO BASIL ZUCCHINI NOODLES
Cooking Time: 15 minutes
Serves: 2
Ingredients:
- 2 medium zucchinis, spiralized into noodles
- 2 tablespoons olive oil
- 2 cloves of garlic, minced
- 200g cherry tomatoes, halved
- 2 tablespoons fresh basil, chopped
- Salt and pepper to taste
- Grated Parmesan cheese for garnish (optional)

Instructions:
1. Heat olive oil in a large frying pan over medium heat. Add minced garlic and sauté for 1-2 minutes until fragrant.
2. Add the spiralized zucchini noodles to the pan and sauté for 2-3 minutes until they are just cooked but still have a slight crunch.
3. Add cherry tomatoes and chopped basil to the pan. Season with salt and pepper. Toss everything together to combine.
4. Cook for an additional 1-2 minutes until the tomatoes are heated through.
5. Remove from heat and garnish with grated Parmesan cheese, if desired.
6. Serve the tomato basil zucchini noodles as a light and refreshing main course or as a side dish.

Nutrition Information per Serving:
- Calories: 150 kcal
- Protein: 4g
- Carbohydrates: 10g
- Fat: 12g
- fibre: 3g

RECIPE 18: STUFFED PORTOBELLO MUSHROOMS
Cooking Time: 25 minutes
Serves: 2
Ingredients:
- 4 large Portobello mushrooms
- 200g fresh spinach leaves
- 100g feta cheese, crumbled
- 2 tablespoons olive oil
- 2 cloves of garlic, minced
- Salt and pepper to taste
- Fresh parsley for garnish

Instructions:
1. Preheat the oven to 200°C (180°C fan).
2. Clean the Portobello mushrooms and remove the stems.
3. In a large frying pan, heat olive oil over medium heat. Add minced garlic and sauté for 1-2 minutes until fragrant.
4. Add the fresh spinach leaves to the pan and sauté until wilted.
5. Remove the pan from heat and let the spinach cool slightly. Once cooled, stir in the crumbled feta cheese.
6. Stuff each Portobello mushroom with the spinach and feta mixture. Season with salt and pepper.
7. Place the stuffed mushrooms on a baking sheet lined with parchment paper.
8. Bake in the preheated oven for 20 minutes or until the mushrooms are tender and the cheese is melted.
9. Garnish with fresh parsley before serving.

Nutrition Information per Serving:
- Calories: 200 kcal
- Protein: 8g
- Carbohydrates: 10g
- Fat: 15g
- fibre: 3g

RECIPE 19: THAI BASIL CHICKEN STIR-FRY

Cooking Time: 20 minutes
Serves: 2
Ingredients:
- 2 tablespoons vegetable oil
- 2 cloves of garlic, minced
- 1 red chilli, sliced (adjust according to spice preference)
- 300g chicken breast, thinly sliced
- 1 tablespoon gluten-free soy sauce
- 1 tablespoon fish sauce
- 1 tablespoon oyster sauce
- 1 teaspoon sugar
- 1 cup fresh basil leaves
- Cooked rice, to serve

Instructions:
1. Heat vegetable oil in a frying pan or wok over medium heat.
2. Add minced garlic and sliced chili to the pan. Sauté for 1 minute until fragrant.
3. Add chicken slices to the pan and stir-fry until cooked through.
4. In a small bowl, mix together gluten-free soy sauce, fish sauce, oyster sauce, and sugar. Pour the sauce mixture into the pan with the chicken.
5. Stir-fry for an additional 1-2 minutes until the sauce is well combined with the chicken.
6. Remove the pan from heat and stir in fresh basil leaves.
7. Serve the Thai basil chicken stir-fry over cooked rice.

Nutrition Information per Serving:
- Calories: 400 kcal
- Protein: 30g
- Carbohydrates: 10g
- Fat: 25g
- fibre: 2g

RECIPE 20: GREEK SALAD WITH GRILLED CHICKEN

Cooking Time: 25 minutes
Serves: 2
Ingredients:
- 2 chicken breasts
- 1 tablespoon olive oil
- Salt and pepper to taste
- 1 head of romaine lettuce, chopped
- 1 cucumber, diced
- 200g cherry tomatoes, halved
- 1/2 red onion, thinly sliced
- 100g Kalamata olives, pitted and halved
- 100g feta cheese, crumbled
- Juice of 1 lemon
- 2 tablespoons extra virgin olive oil
- 1 teaspoon dried oregano

Instructions:
1. Preheat a grill or grill pan over medium-high heat.
2. Rub the chicken breasts with olive oil, salt, and pepper.
3. Grill the chicken for about 6-7 minutes per side, or until cooked through.
4. Remove the chicken from the grill and let it rest for a few minutes. Slice the chicken into thin strips.
5. In a large bowl, combine romaine lettuce, diced cucumber, cherry tomatoes, sliced red onion, Kalamata olives, and crumbled feta cheese.

6. In a small bowl, whisk together lemon juice, extra virgin olive oil, dried oregano, salt, and pepper to make the dressing.
7. Pour the dressing over the salad and toss to combine.
8. Divide the salad onto plates and top with the grilled chicken slices.
9. Serve the Greek salad with grilled chicken as a refreshing and light main course.

Nutrition Information per Serving:
- Calories: 400 kcal
- Protein: 35g
- Carbohydrates: 15g
- Fat: 20g
- Fiber: 5g

RECIPE 21: QUINOA STUFFED BUTTERNUT SQUASH

Cooking Time: 45 minutes
Serves: 4
Ingredients:
- 1 medium butternut squash
- 1 cup quinoa
- 2 cups vegetable broth
- 1 tablespoon olive oil
- 1 small onion, finely chopped
- 2 cloves of garlic, minced
- 1 red bell pepper, diced
- 1 zucchini, diced
- 1 carrot, diced
- 1 teaspoon dried thyme
- Salt and pepper to taste
- Fresh parsley for garnish

Instructions:
1. Preheat the oven to 200°C (180°C fan).
2. Slice the butternut squash in half lengthwise and scoop out the seeds and membranes.
3. Place the butternut squash halves on a baking sheet, cut side down. Bake for 30-35 minutes until the squash is tender when pierced with a fork.
4. While the squash is baking, cook the quinoa according to package instructions, using vegetable broth instead of water.
5. In a large frying pan, heat olive oil over medium heat. Add chopped onion and minced garlic. Sauté until the onion is translucent and fragrant.
6. Add diced red bell pepper, zucchini, carrot, dried thyme, salt, and pepper to the pan. Sauté for 5-7 minutes until the vegetables are tender.
7. Once the quinoa and vegetables are cooked, combine them in a large bowl. Stir to mix well.
8. Remove the baked butternut squash from the oven. Fill each squash half with the quinoa and vegetable mixture.
9. Return the stuffed butternut squash halves to the oven and bake for an additional 10 minutes.
10. Garnish with fresh parsley before serving.

Nutrition Information per Serving:
- Calories: 300 kcal
- Protein: 10g
- Carbohydrates: 60g
- Fat: 4g
- fibre: 10g

RECIPE 22: PESTO CHICKEN WITH ROASTED VEGETABLES

Cooking Time: 30 minutes
Serves: 2
Ingredients:
- 2 chicken breasts
- 3 tablespoons gluten-free pesto
- 2 tablespoons olive oil
- 200g cherry tomatoes
- 1 red onion, cut into wedges
- 1 red bell pepper, sliced

- 1 courgette, sliced
- Salt and pepper to taste
- Fresh basil leaves for garnish

Instructions:
1. Preheat the oven to 200°C (180°C fan).
2. Place the chicken breasts in a bowl and coat them with gluten-free pesto. Let them marinate for 10 minutes.
3. In a separate bowl, combine olive oil, cherry tomatoes, red onion wedges, red bell pepper slices, courgette slices, salt, and pepper. Toss to coat the vegetables.
4. Place the marinated chicken breasts and the vegetable mixture on a baking sheet lined with parchment paper.
5. Bake in the preheated oven for 20-25 minutes, or until the chicken is cooked through and the vegetables are tender.
6. Garnish with fresh basil leaves before serving.

Nutrition Information per Serving:
- Calories: 350 kcal
- Protein: 30g
- Carbohydrates: 15g
- Fat: 18g
- fibre: 4g

RECIPE 23: MEXICAN QUINOA STUFFED PEPPERS

Cooking Time: 45 minutes
Serves: 4
Ingredients:
- 4 bell peppers (any colour)
- 200g quinoa
- 400g canned black beans, drained and rinsed
- 200g canned diced tomatoes
- 1 small onion, finely chopped
- 2 cloves of garlic, minced
- 1 teaspoon ground cumin
- 1 teaspoon chilli powder
- Salt and pepper to taste
- 100g shredded cheddar cheese (optional)
- Fresh coriander for garnish

Instructions:
1. Preheat the oven to 200°C (180°C fan).
2. Cut off the tops of the bell peppers and remove the seeds and membranes. Set them aside.
3. In a saucepan, cook the quinoa according to package instructions.
4. In a separate pan, sauté the onion and garlic until softened. Add the canned diced tomatoes, black beans, ground cumin, chilli powder, salt, and pepper. Cook for a few minutes to heat through.
5. Combine the cooked quinoa with the bean and tomato mixture.
6. Stuff each bell pepper with the quinoa and bean filling.
7. Place the stuffed peppers in a baking dish. If desired, sprinkle shredded cheddar cheese on top of each pepper.
8. Bake in the preheated oven for 25-30 minutes or until the peppers are tender and the cheese is melted and bubbly.
9. Garnish with fresh coriander before serving.

Nutrition Information per Serving:
- Calories: 300 kcal
- Protein: 12g
- Carbohydrates: 55g
- Fat: 4g
- fibre: 12g

RECIPE 24: LEMON GARLIC SHRIMP SKEWERS
Cooking Time: 15 minutes
Serves: 2
Ingredients:
- 300g shrimp, peeled and deveined
- 2 tablespoons olive oil
- 2 cloves of garlic, minced
- Zest and juice of 1 lemon
- Salt and pepper to taste
- Fresh parsley for garnish

Instructions:
1. Preheat the grill or grill pan over medium-high heat.
2. In a bowl, combine olive oil, minced garlic, lemon zest, lemon juice, salt, and pepper. Mix well.
3. Thread the shrimp onto skewers.
4. Brush the shrimp skewers with the lemon garlic mixture, coating them evenly.
5. Grill the shrimp skewers for 2-3 minutes per side, or until they are cooked through and opaque.
6. Remove the skewers from the grill and garnish with fresh parsley.
7. Serve the lemon garlic shrimp skewers with a side of salad or grilled vegetables.

Nutrition Information per Serving:
- Calories: 200 kcal
- Protein: 25g
- Carbohydrates: 2g
- Fat: 10g
- fibre: 0g

RECIPE 25: BAKED LEMON HERB SALMON
Cooking Time: 20 minutes
Serves: 2
Ingredients:
- 2 salmon fillets
- 2 tablespoons olive oil
- Zest and juice of 1 lemon
- 1 teaspoon dried dill
- 1 teaspoon dried parsley
- Salt and pepper to taste
- Lemon slices for garnish

Instructions:
1. Preheat the oven to 200°C (180°C fan).
2. Place the salmon fillets on a baking sheet lined with parchment paper.
3. In a small bowl, combine olive oil, lemon zest, lemon juice, dried dill, dried parsley, salt, and pepper. Mix well.
4. Brush the lemon herb mixture onto the salmon fillets, coating them evenly.
5. Place lemon slices on top of each salmon fillet.
6. Bake in the preheated oven for 15-20 minutes, or until the salmon is cooked through and flakes easily with a fork.
7. Serve the baked lemon herb salmon with a side of steamed vegetables or salad.

Nutrition Information per Serving:
- Calories: 300 kcal
- Protein: 25g
- Carbohydrates: 2g
- Fat: 20g
- fibre: 0g

RECIPE 26: QUINOA AND VEGETABLE STIR-FRY

Cooking Time: 25 minutes
Serves: 2
Ingredients:

- 1 cup quinoa
- 2 cups vegetable broth
- 2 tablespoons olive oil
- 1 small onion, thinly sliced
- 1 red bell pepper, thinly sliced
- 1 courgette, thinly sliced
- 100g sugar snap peas
- 2 cloves of garlic, minced
- 2 tablespoons gluten-free soy sauce
- Salt and pepper to taste
- Fresh coriander for garnish

Instructions:

1. Rinse the quinoa under cold water. Cook the quinoa according to package instructions, using vegetable broth instead of water.
2. Heat olive oil in a large frying pan or wok over medium heat. Add thinly sliced onion, red bell pepper, courgette, sugar snap peas, and minced garlic.
3. Stir-fry the vegetables for 5-7 minutes until they are tender-crisp.
4. Add the cooked quinoa to the pan and pour gluten-free soy sauce over the mixture. Stir everything together to combine.
5. Cook for another 2-3 minutes until heated through.
6. Season with salt and pepper to taste.
7. Garnish with fresh coriander before serving.

Nutrition Information per Serving:

- Calories: 350 kcal
- Protein: 8g
- Carbohydrates: 50g
- Fat: 15g
- fibre: 8g

RECIPE 27: ZUCCHINI NOODLES WITH TOMATO SAUCE

Cooking Time: 20 minutes
Serves: 2
Ingredients:

- 2 large zucchinis
- 2 tablespoons olive oil
- 2 cloves of garlic, minced
- 400g canned diced tomatoes
- 1 teaspoon dried basil
- 1 teaspoon dried oregano
- Salt and pepper to taste
- Grated Parmesan cheese for garnish (optional)

Instructions:

1. Spiralized the zucchinis into noodles using a spiralized.
2. Heat olive oil in a large frying pan over medium heat. Add minced garlic and sauté for 1-2 minutes until fragrant.
3. Add canned diced tomatoes, dried basil, dried oregano, salt, and pepper to the pan. Stir to combine.
4. Simmer the tomato sauce for 10-15 minutes, stirring occasionally, until it has thickened slightly and the flavours have melded together.
5. In a separate pan, heat a little olive oil over medium heat. Add the zucchini noodles and sauté for 3-4 minutes until they are tender-crisp.
6. Divide the zucchini noodles onto plates and top with the tomato sauce.
7. If desired, sprinkle grated Parmesan cheese on top.
8. Serve the zucchini noodles with tomato sauce as a light and gluten-free pasta alternative.

Nutrition Information per Serving:
- Calories: 200 kcal
- Protein: 4g
- Carbohydrates: 15g
- Fat: 15g
- Fiber: 5g

RECIPE 28: HONEY MUSTARD CHICKEN WITH ROASTED VEGETABLES

Cooking Time: 30 minutes
Serves: 2
Ingredients:
- 2 chicken breasts
- 2 tablespoons Dijon mustard
- 2 tablespoons honey
- 1 tablespoon olive oil
- 1 tablespoon apple cider vinegar
- Salt and pepper to taste
- 200g baby potatoes, halved
- 200g broccoli florets
- 1 red onion, cut into wedges
- Fresh parsley for garnish

Instructions:
1. Preheat the oven to 200°C (180°C fan).
2. In a small bowl, whisk together Dijon mustard, honey, olive oil, apple cider vinegar, salt, and pepper.
3. Place the chicken breasts in a baking dish and brush them with the honey mustard mixture, coating them evenly.
4. In a separate bowl, toss baby potatoes, broccoli florets, and red onion wedges with olive oil, salt, and pepper.
5. Arrange the vegetables around the chicken breasts in the baking dish.
6. Bake in the preheated oven for 25-30 minutes, or until the chicken is cooked through and the vegetables are tender.
7. Garnish with fresh parsley before serving.

Nutrition Information per Serving:
- Calories: 350 kcal
- Protein: 30g
- Carbohydrates: 30g
- Fat: 12g
- fibre: 5g

RECIPE 29: QUINOA STUFFED MUSHROOMS

Cooking Time: 25 minutes
Serves: 4
Ingredients:
- 8 large mushrooms
- 1 cup quinoa
- 2 cups vegetable broth
- 1 tablespoon olive oil
- 1 small onion, finely chopped
- 2 cloves of garlic, minced
- 1 red bell pepper, finely chopped
- 1 carrot, finely chopped
- 1 teaspoon dried thyme
- Salt and pepper to taste
- Fresh parsley for garnish

Instructions:
1. Preheat the oven to 200°C (180°C fan).
2. Clean the mushrooms and remove the stems. Set them aside.
3. Rinse the quinoa under cold water. Cook the quinoa according to package instructions, using vegetable broth instead of water.
4. In a frying pan, heat olive oil over medium heat. Add chopped onion, minced garlic, red bell pepper, carrot, dried thyme, salt, and pepper. Sauté until the vegetables are tender.

5. Combine the cooked quinoa with the sautéed vegetable mixture.
6. Spoon the quinoa mixture into each mushroom cap, filling it generously.
7. Place the stuffed mushrooms on a baking sheet lined with parchment paper.
8. Bake in the preheated oven for 20 minutes or until the mushrooms are tender and the filling is lightly browned.
9. Garnish with fresh parsley before serving.

Nutrition Information per Serving:
- Calories: 200 kcal
- Protein: 8g
- Carbohydrates: 35g
- Fat: 4g
- fibre: 6g

Recipe 30: Shrimp and Vegetable Stir-Fry
Cooking Time: 20 minutes
Serves: 2
Ingredients:
- 300g shrimp, peeled and deveined
- 2 tablespoons gluten-free soy sauce
- 1 tablespoon honey
- 1 tablespoon rice vinegar
- 1 tablespoon olive oil
- 1 red bell pepper, thinly sliced
- 1 yellow bell pepper, thinly sliced
- 1 courgette, thinly sliced
- 1 carrot, thinly sliced
- 2 cloves of garlic, minced
- 1 teaspoon grated ginger
- 2 spring onions, sliced
- Sesame seeds for garnish

Instructions:
1. In a small bowl, whisk together gluten-free soy sauce, honey, rice vinegar, and olive oil. Set aside.
2. Heat olive oil in a large frying pan or wok over medium-high heat. Add the shrimp and cook until pink and cooked through. Remove from the pan and set aside.
3. In the same pan, add a little more oil if needed and sauté the bell peppers, courgette, carrot, minced garlic, and grated ginger for 3-4 minutes until the vegetables are tender-crisp.
4. Return the cooked shrimp to the pan and pour the sauce over the ingredients. Toss everything together to coat.
5. Cook for an additional 2-3 minutes until heated through.
6. Garnish with sliced spring onions and sprinkle with sesame seeds before serving.
7. Serve the shrimp and vegetable stir-fry over cooked rice or noodles.

Nutrition Information per Serving:
- Calories: 300 kcal
- Protein: 25g
- Carbohydrates: 25g
- Fat: 10g
- fibre: 5g

Please note that the nutrition information provided is approximate and may vary depending on specific ingredients and brands used.

Gluten-Free Dessert Recipes

Recipe 1: Chocolate Mug Cake
Cooking Time: 5 minutes
Serving: 1 mug cake
Ingredients:
- 4 tablespoons gluten-free self-rising flour
- 2 tablespoons cocoa powder
- 2 tablespoons granulated sugar
- 1/4 teaspoon baking powder
- 3 tablespoons milk
- 2 tablespoons vegetable oil
- 1/4 teaspoon vanilla extract
- 1 tablespoon chocolate chips (optional)

Instructions:
1. In a microwave-safe mug, combine the gluten-free self-rising flour, cocoa powder, granulated sugar, and baking powder.
2. Add the milk, vegetable oil, and vanilla extract to the mug. Stir until well combined and no lumps remain.
3. If desired, sprinkle chocolate chips on top of the batter.
4. Microwave the mug on high for 1 minute and 30 seconds, or until the cake has risen and is set in the middle.
5. Carefully remove the mug from the microwave (it will be hot). Allow it to cool for a minute or two before enjoying.

Nutrition Information (per serving):
- Calories: 300
- Protein: 4g
- Carbohydrates: 38g
- Fat: 16g
- fibre: 3g

Recipe 2: Strawberry Spinach Salad
Cooking Time: 15 minutes
Serving: 4 servings
Ingredients:
- 4 cups baby spinach leaves
- 1 cup fresh strawberries, sliced
- 1/4 cup feta cheese, crumbled
- 2 tablespoons sliced almonds
- 2 tablespoons balsamic vinegar
- 1 tablespoon extra-virgin olive oil
- 1 teaspoon honey
- Salt and pepper to taste

Instructions:
1. In a large bowl, combine the baby spinach, sliced strawberries, feta cheese, and sliced almonds.
2. In a small bowl, whisk together the balsamic vinegar, extra-virgin olive oil, honey, salt, and pepper until well combined.
3. Pour the dressing over the salad and toss gently to coat.
4. Serve immediately as a refreshing and nutritious side dish.

Nutrition Information (per serving):
- Calories: 180
- Protein: 4g
- Carbohydrates: 12g
- Fat: 13g
- Fiber: 3g

RECIPE 3: HONEY GLAZED SALMON

Cooking Time: 20 minutes
Serving: 2 servings
Ingredients:

- 2 salmon fillets
- 2 tablespoons gluten-free soy sauce
- 1 tablespoon honey
- 1 tablespoon lemon juice
- 1/2 teaspoon minced garlic
- Salt and pepper to taste
- Chopped fresh parsley for garnish

Instructions:

1. Preheat the oven to 200°C (180°C fan) or 400°F (350°F fan).
2. In a small bowl, whisk together the gluten-free soy sauce, honey, lemon juice, minced garlic, salt, and pepper.
3. Place the salmon fillets on a baking sheet lined with parchment paper.
4. Brush the honey glaze mixture over the salmon fillets, making sure to coat them evenly.
5. Bake the salmon in the preheated oven for 15-18 minutes, or until the fish is cooked through and flakes easily with a fork.
6. Garnish with chopped fresh parsley before serving.

Nutrition Information (per serving):

- Calories: 300
- Protein: 24g
- Carbohydrates: 10g
- Fat: 18g
- fibre: 0g

RECIPE 4: QUINOA STUFFED BELL PEPPERS

Cooking Time: 30 minutes
Serving: 4 servings
Ingredients:

- 4 bell peppers (any colour)
- 1 cup cooked quinoa
- 1 cup black beans, rinsed and drained
- 1/2 cup corn kernels
- 1/2 cup diced tomatoes
- 1/4 cup diced red onion
- 1/4 cup chopped fresh cilantro
- 1 tablespoon lime juice
- 1 teaspoon ground cumin
- 1/2 teaspoon chilli powder
- Salt and pepper to taste
- Grated cheddar cheese (optional)

Instructions:

1. Preheat the oven to 200°C (180°C fan) or 400°F (350°F fan).
2. Cut off the tops of the bell peppers and remove the seeds and membranes.
3. In a mixing bowl, combine the cooked quinoa, black beans, corn kernels, diced tomatoes, red onion, cilantro, lime juice, ground cumin, chilli powder, salt, and pepper. Stir well to combine.
4. Stuff each bell pepper with the quinoa mixture, pressing it down lightly.
5. Place the stuffed bell peppers in a baking dish and cover with foil.
6. Bake in the preheated oven for 20 minutes.
7. If desired, remove the foil, sprinkle grated cheddar cheese on top of each bell pepper, and bake for an additional 5 minutes, or until the cheese is melted and bubbly.
8. Serve hot as a satisfying and flavourful main dish.

Nutrition Information (per serving):

- Calories: 250
- Protein: 10g
- Carbohydrates: 47g
- Fat: 2g
- fibre: 10g

RECIPE 5: APPLE CINNAMON OATMEAL
Cooking Time: 15 minutes
Ingredients:
- 1 cup gluten-free rolled oats
- 2 cups water
- 1 apple, peeled, cored, and chopped
- 1 tablespoon maple syrup
- 1/2 teaspoon ground cinnamon
- 1/4 teaspoon vanilla extract
- Chopped nuts or raisins for topping (optional)

Instructions:
1. In a medium saucepan, combine the gluten-free rolled oats and water.
2. Bring the mixture to a boil over medium heat, then reduce the heat to low and simmer for about 10 minutes, stirring occasionally.
3. Add the chopped apple, maple syrup, ground cinnamon, and vanilla extract to the saucepan. Stir well to combine.
4. Continue cooking for another 3-5 minutes or until the oats are tender and the apple is soft.
5. Remove from heat and let it sit for a minute or two.
6. Serve the apple cinnamon oatmeal hot, topped with chopped nuts or raisins if desired.

Nutrition Information (per serving):
- Calories: 200
- Protein: 4g
- Carbohydrates: 42g
- Fat: 3g
- fibre: 6g

RECIPE 6: CAPRESE SKEWERS
Cooking Time: 15 minutes
Ingredients:
- 8 cherry tomatoes
- 8 small mozzarella balls
- 8 fresh basil leaves
- 2 tablespoons balsamic glaze
- Salt and pepper to taste

Instructions:
1. Thread a cherry tomato, mozzarella ball, and basil leaf onto a skewer. Repeat with the remaining ingredients to make a total of 8 skewers.
2. Arrange the skewers on a serving plate.
3. Drizzle the balsamic glaze over the skewers.
4. Season with salt and pepper to taste.
5. Serve the Caprese skewers as a delightful appetizer or snack.

Nutrition Information (per serving - 2 skewers):
- Calories: 120
- Protein: 8g
- Carbohydrates: 5g
- Fat: 8g
- fibre: 0g

RECIPE 7: CHICKPEA SALAD
Cooking Time: 10 minutes
Ingredients:
- 1 can chickpeas, rinsed and drained
- 1/2 cucumber, diced
- 1/2 red bell pepper, diced
- 1/4 cup diced red onion
- 2 tablespoons chopped fresh parsley
- 2 tablespoons lemon juice
- 1 tablespoon extra-virgin olive oil
- Salt and pepper to taste

Instructions:

1. In a large bowl, combine the chickpeas, diced cucumber, diced red bell pepper, diced red onion, and chopped fresh parsley.
2. In a small bowl, whisk together the lemon juice, extra-virgin olive oil, salt, and pepper.
3. Pour the dressing over the chickpea mixture and toss well to combine.
4. Adjust the seasoning if needed.
5. Serve the chickpea salad as a light and nutritious side dish or a filling main course.

Nutrition Information (per serving):
- Calories: 180
- Protein: 7g
- Carbohydrates: 25g
- Fat: 6g
- fibre: 7g

RECIPE 8: GLUTEN-FREE BANANA PANCAKES

Cooking Time: 20 minutes
Ingredients:
- 1 cup gluten-free all-purpose flour
- 1 tablespoon granulated sugar
- 1 teaspoon baking powder
- 1/2 teaspoon baking soda
- 1/4 teaspoon salt
- 1 ripe banana, mashed
- 1 cup buttermilk
- 1 large egg
- 1 tablespoon vegetable oil
- Optional toppings: sliced bananas, maple syrup, chopped nuts

Instructions:
1. In a mixing bowl, whisk together the gluten-free all-purpose flour, granulated sugar, baking powder, baking soda, and salt.
1. In a separate bowl, mash the ripe banana until smooth. Add the buttermilk, egg, and vegetable oil to the banana and whisk until well combined.
2. Pour the wet ingredients into the dry ingredients and stir until just combined. Do not overmix; a few lumps are fine.
3. Heat a non-stick skillet or griddle over medium heat and lightly grease with oil or cooking spray.
4. Pour about 1/4 cup of the pancake batter onto the skillet for each pancake.
5. Cook until bubbles form on the surface of the pancake, then flip and cook for another 1-2 minutes until golden brown.
6. Repeat with the remaining batter.
7. Serve the gluten-free banana pancakes warm with your choice of toppings, such as sliced bananas, maple syrup, or chopped nuts.

Nutrition Information (per serving - without toppings):
- Calories: 200
- Protein: 5g
- Carbohydrates: 33g
- Fat: 6g
- fibre: 2g

RECIPE 9: MEDITERRANEAN QUINOA SALAD

Cooking Time: 25 minutes
Ingredients:
- 1 cup cooked quinoa
- 1 cup cherry tomatoes, halved
- 1/2 cucumber, diced
- 1/2 red bell pepper, diced
- 1/4 cup diced red onion
- 1/4 cup sliced black olives
- 2 tablespoons chopped fresh parsley
- 2 tablespoons lemon juice

- 1 tablespoon extra-virgin olive oil
- 1/2 teaspoon dried oregano
- Salt and pepper to taste
- Feta cheese for topping (optional)

Instructions:
1. In a large bowl, combine the cooked quinoa, cherry tomatoes, diced cucumber, diced red bell pepper, diced red onion, sliced black olives, and chopped fresh parsley.
2. In a small bowl, whisk together the lemon juice, extra-virgin olive oil, dried oregano, salt, and pepper.
3. Pour the dressing over the quinoa mixture and toss well to combine.
4. Adjust the seasoning if needed.
5. Sprinkle feta cheese on top before serving, if desired.
6. Serve the Mediterranean quinoa salad as a refreshing and protein-packed side dish or a light main course.

Nutrition Information (per serving):
- Calories: 220
- Protein: 6g
- Carbohydrates: 31g
- Fat: 8g
- fibre: 5g

RECIPE 10: GLUTEN-FREE LEMON BARS

Cooking Time: 45 minutes
Ingredients:
For the crust:
- 1 cup gluten-free all-purpose flour
- 1/4 cup powdered sugar
- 1/2 cup unsalted butter, softened

For the filling:
- 3/4 cup granulated sugar
- 2 tablespoons gluten-free all-purpose flour
- 1/4 teaspoon baking powder
- 2 large eggs
- Zest and juice of 2 lemons
- Powdered sugar for dusting

Instructions:
1. Preheat the oven to 180°C (160°C fan) or 350°F (320°F fan). Grease an 8x8-inch baking dish.
2. In a mixing bowl, combine the gluten-free all-purpose flour and powdered sugar for the crust. Add the softened butter and mix until the mixture resembles coarse crumbs.
3. Press the crust mixture evenly into the bottom of the greased baking dish.
4. Bake the crust in the preheated oven for 15-18 minutes, or until lightly golden brown.
5. Meanwhile, prepare the filling by whisking together the granulated sugar, gluten-free all-purpose flour, and baking powder in a bowl.
6. In a separate bowl, beat the eggs and then add the lemon zest and juice. Mix well.
7. Add the egg mixture to the dry ingredients and whisk until well combined.
8. Pour the filling mixture over the baked crust.
9. Bake in the oven for an additional 20-25 minutes, or until the filling is set.
10. Remove from the oven and let the lemon bars cool completely in the baking dish.
11. Once cooled, dust the top with powdered sugar.
12. Cut into squares and serve as a tangy and sweet gluten-free dessert.

Nutrition Information (per serving):
- Calories: 180
- Protein: 2g
- Carbohydrates: 25g
- Fat: 8g
- fibre: 0g

RECIPE 11: QUINOA STIR-FRY

Cooking Time: 25 minutes

Ingredients:
- 1 cup cooked quinoa
- 1 tablespoon vegetable oil
- 1/2 onion, sliced
- 1 bell pepper, sliced
- 1 carrot, julienned
- 1/2 cup snow peas
- 2 cloves garlic, minced
- 2 tablespoons gluten-free soy sauce
- 1 tablespoon sesame oil
- 1/2 teaspoon ground ginger
- Salt and pepper to taste
- Chopped green onions for garnish

Instructions:
1. Heat the vegetable oil in a large skillet or wok over medium-high heat.
2. Add the sliced onion, bell pepper, carrot, and snow peas to the skillet. Stir-fry for 3-4 minutes until the vegetables are crisp-tender.
3. Add the minced garlic to the skillet and stir-fry for an additional 1 minute.
4. Push the vegetables to one side of the skillet and add the cooked quinoa to the other side.
5. In a small bowl, whisk together the gluten-free soy sauce, sesame oil, ground ginger, salt, and pepper.
6. Pour the sauce over the quinoa and stir to coat the quinoa and vegetables evenly.
7. Continue stir-frying for 2-3 minutes until everything is heated through.
8. Remove from heat and garnish with chopped green onions.
9. Serve the quinoa stir-fry as a flavourful and nutritious main dish.

Nutrition Information (per serving):
- Calories: 250
- Protein: 6g
- Carbohydrates: 31g
- Fat: 11g
- Fiber: 5g

Gluten-Free Seafood Recipes

Recipe 1: Lemon Garlic Shrimp
Cooking Time: 20 minutes
Serves: 2
Ingredients:
- 250g shrimp, peeled and deveined
- 2 tablespoons olive oil
- 2 cloves garlic, minced
- 1 lemon, juiced
- Salt and pepper to taste
- Fresh parsley, chopped (for garnish)

Instructions:
1. Heat olive oil in a large skillet over medium heat.
2. Add minced garlic and sauté for 1 minute until fragrant.
3. Add shrimp to the skillet and cook for 3-4 minutes, or until they turn pink.
4. Squeeze the juice of one lemon over the shrimp.
5. Season with salt and pepper to taste.
6. Cook for another 2 minutes until the shrimp are cooked through.
7. Garnish with fresh parsley and serve hot.

Nutrition Information (per serving):
- Calories: 250
- Protein: 25g
- Fat: 15g
- Carbohydrates: 5g
- fibre: 1g

Recipe 2: Baked Salmon with Herb Crust
Cooking Time: 25 minutes
Serves: 2
Ingredients:
- 2 salmon fillets (about 180g each)
- 2 tablespoons gluten-free breadcrumbs
- 1 tablespoon fresh parsley, chopped
- 1 tablespoon fresh dill, chopped
- 1 tablespoon fresh chives, chopped
- 1 tablespoon olive oil
- Salt and pepper to taste
- Lemon wedges (for serving)

Instructions:
1. Preheat the oven to 200°C (180°C fan-assisted) or 400°F.
2. Place the salmon fillets on a baking sheet lined with parchment paper.
3. In a small bowl, combine the gluten-free breadcrumbs, chopped parsley, dill, chives, olive oil, salt, and pepper.
4. Press the herb mixture onto the top of each salmon fillet, creating a crust.
5. Bake in the preheated oven for 15-18 minutes, or until the salmon is cooked to your desired level of doneness.
6. Serve hot with lemon wedges.

Nutrition Information (per serving):
- Calories: 350
- Protein: 30g
- Fat: 20g
- Carbohydrates: 5g
- fibre: 1g

RECIPE 3: GRILLED GARLIC BUTTER PRAWNS

Cooking Time: 15 minutes
Serves: 2
Ingredients:
- 300g prawns, peeled and deveined
- 2 tablespoons butter, melted
- 2 cloves garlic, minced
- Lemon wedges (for serving)
- 1 tablespoon fresh parsley, chopped
- Salt and pepper to taste

Instructions:
1. Preheat the grill to medium-high heat.
2. In a small bowl, combine the melted butter, minced garlic, chopped parsley, salt, and pepper.
3. Thread the prawns onto skewers, piercing through the tail and head.
4. Brush the garlic butter mixture over the prawns, ensuring they are well-coated.
5. Place the prawn skewers on the grill and cook for 2-3 minutes on each side, or until they turn pink and opaque.
6. Remove from the grill and serve hot with lemon wedges.

Nutrition Information (per serving):
- Calories: 200
- Protein: 25g
- Fat: 10g
- Carbohydrates: 2g
- fibre: 0g

RECIPE 4: THAI COCONUT CURRY SHRIMP

Cooking Time: 30 minutes
Serves: 4
Ingredients:
- 500g shrimp, peeled and deveined
- 1 tablespoon coconut oil
- 1 onion, chopped
- 2 cloves garlic, minced
- 1 red bell pepper, sliced
- 1 green bell pepper, sliced
- 1 tablespoon Thai red curry paste
- 400ml can coconut milk
- 1 tablespoon fish sauce (ensure it's gluten-free)
- 1 tablespoon lime juice
- Fresh cilantro, chopped (for garnish)
- Cooked rice or rice noodles (to serve)

Instructions:
1. Heat coconut oil in a large pan over medium heat.
2. Add chopped onion and minced garlic. Sauté for 2-3 minutes until fragrant.
3. Add sliced bell peppers and cook for another 2 minutes.
4. Push the vegetables to one side of the pan and add the Thai red curry paste. Stir and cook for 1 minute.
5. Add shrimp to the pan and cook for 2-3 minutes until they start to turn pink.
6. Pour in the coconut milk and fish sauce. Stir well to combine.
7. Simmer for 10-15 minutes, stirring occasionally, until the shrimp are cooked through and the sauce has thickened slightly.
8. Stir in lime juice.
9. Serve the curry over cooked rice or rice noodles, garnished with fresh cilantro.

Nutrition Information (per serving):
- Calories: 350
- Protein: 25g

- Fat: 20g
- Carbohydrates: 15g
- Fiber: 2g

RECIPE 5: GRILLED LEMON HERB SEA BASS
Cooking Time: 20 minutes
Serves: 2
Ingredients:
- 2 sea bass fillets (about 180g each)
- 2 tablespoons olive oil
- 2 cloves garlic, minced
- Zest of 1 lemon
- 1 tablespoon fresh thyme leaves
- Salt and pepper to taste
- Lemon wedges (for serving

Instructions:
1. Preheat the grill to medium-high heat.
2. In a small bowl, combine olive oil, minced garlic, lemon zest, thyme leaves, salt, and pepper.
3. Brush the mixture over both sides of the sea bass fillets.
4. Place the fillets on the grill and cook for 4-5 minutes per side, or until the fish flakes easily with a fork and has a lightly charred exterior.
5. Remove from the grill and squeeze fresh lemon juice over the fillets.
6. Serve hot with additional lemon wedges.

Nutrition Information (per serving):
- Calories: 300
- Protein: 30g
- Fat: 18g
- Carbohydrates: 2g
- fibre: 0g

RECIPE 6: BAKED COD WITH TOMATO AND OLIVE SALSA
Cooking Time: 25 minutes
Serves: 4
Ingredients:
- 4 cod fillets (about 150g each)
- 2 tablespoons olive oil
- 2 tomatoes, diced
- 1/4 cup pitted black olives, sliced
- 1/4 cup fresh basil leaves, chopped
- 1 tablespoon red wine vinegar
- Salt and pepper to taste
- Lemon wedges (for serving)

Instructions:
- Preheat the oven to 200°C (180°C fan-assisted) or 400°F.
- Place the cod fillets on a baking sheet lined with parchment paper.
- Drizzle the fillets with olive oil and season with salt and pepper.
- Bake in the preheated oven for 15-18 minutes, or until the fish is opaque and flakes easily with a fork.
- In a bowl, combine the diced tomatoes, sliced olives, chopped basil leaves, red wine vinegar, salt, and pepper. Toss well to combine.
- Serve the baked cod topped with the tomato and olive salsa. Garnish with lemon wedges.

Nutrition Information (per serving):
- Calories: 250
- Protein: 25g
- Fat: 12g
- Carbohydrates: 6g
- fibre: 2g

RECIPE 7: GARLIC LIME GRILLED PRAWNS

Cooking Time: 15 minutes
Serves: 4
Ingredients:
- 500g prawns, peeled and deveined
- 3 cloves garlic, minced
- Zest and juice of 2 limes
- 2 tablespoons olive oil
- 1 tablespoon fresh cilantro, chopped
- Salt and pepper to taste

Instructions:
1. In a bowl, combine the minced garlic, lime zest, lime juice, olive oil, chopped cilantro, salt, and pepper.
2. Add the prawns to the bowl and toss to coat them in the marinade. Let them marinate for 10 minutes.
3. Preheat the grill to medium-high heat.
4. Thread the prawns onto skewers, piercing through the tail and head.
5. Place the prawn skewers on the grill and cook for 2-3 minutes on each side, or until they turn pink and opaque.
6. Remove from the grill and serve hot.

Nutrition Information (per serving):
- Calories: 200
- Protein: 25g
- Fat: 9g
- Carbohydrates: 4g
- fibre: 0g

RECIPE 8: GRILLED CAJUN SHRIMP SKEWERS

Cooking Time: 20 minutes
Serves: 4
Ingredients:
- 500g large shrimp, peeled and deveined
- 2 tablespoons olive oil
- 1 tablespoon Cajun seasoning (ensure it's gluten-free)
- 1 teaspoon paprika
- 1/2 teaspoon garlic powder
- 1/2 teaspoon onion powder
- 1/2 teaspoon dried thyme
- Salt and pepper to taste
- Lemon wedges (for serving)

Instructions:
1. Preheat the grill to medium-high heat.
2. In a bowl, combine the olive oil, Cajun seasoning, paprika, garlic powder, onion powder, dried thyme, salt, and pepper.
3. Add the shrimp to the bowl and toss to coat them evenly with the spice mixture.
4. Thread the shrimp onto skewers, piercing through the tail and head.
5. Place the shrimp skewers on the grill and cook for 2-3 minutes on each side, or until they turn pink and opaque.
6. Remove from the grill and serve hot with lemon wedges.

Nutrition Information (per serving):
- Calories: 180
- Protein: 25g
- Fat: 8g
- Carbohydrates: 1g
- fibre: 0g

RECIPE 9: BAKED LEMON HERB SALMON
Cooking Time: 25 minutes
Serves: 4
Ingredients:
- 4 salmon fillets (about 150g each)
- 2 tablespoons olive oil
- Zest and juice of 1 lemon
- 2 tablespoons fresh dill, chopped
- 2 tablespoons fresh parsley, chopped
- Salt and pepper to taste
- Lemon wedges (for serving)

Instructions:
1. Preheat the oven to 200°C (180°C fan-assisted) or 400°F.
2. Place the salmon fillets on a baking sheet lined with parchment paper.
3. Drizzle the fillets with olive oil and season with salt and pepper.
4. Sprinkle the lemon zest, lemon juice, fresh dill, and fresh parsley over the fillets.
5. Bake in the preheated oven for 15-18 minutes, or until the salmon is cooked to your desired level of doneness.
6. Serve hot with lemon wedges.

Nutrition Information (per serving):
- Calories: 300
- Protein: 25g
- Fat: 20g
- Carbohydrates: 1g
- fibre: 0g

RECIPE 10: BAKED GARLIC HERB SCALLOPS
Cooking Time: 15 minutes
Serves: 4
Ingredients:
- 500g scallops
- 2 tablespoons olive oil
- 3 cloves garlic, minced
- 1 tablespoon fresh parsley, chopped
- 1 tablespoon fresh thyme leaves
- Salt and pepper to taste
- Lemon wedges (for serving)

Instructions:
1. Preheat the oven to 220°C (200°C fan-assisted) or 425°F.
2. Place the scallops in a baking dish.
3. In a small bowl, combine the olive oil, minced garlic, chopped parsley, thyme leaves, salt, and pepper.
4. Drizzle the garlic herb mixture over the scallops, ensuring they are well-coated.
5. Bake in the preheated oven for 10-12 minutes, or until the scallops are opaque and cooked through.
6. Serve hot with lemon wedges.

Nutrition Information (per serving):
- Calories: 180
- Protein: 25g
- Fat: 8g
- Carbohydrates: 3g
- fibre: 0g

RECIPE 11: TUNA AVOCADO LETTUCE WRAPS
Preparation Time: 15 minutes
Serves: 2
Ingredients:
- 2 cans tuna in water, drained
- 1 avocado, diced
- 2 tablespoons mayonnaise (ensure its gluten-free)
- 1 tablespoon fresh lemon juice
- 2 tablespoons chopped red onion
- 2 tablespoons chopped fresh cilantro
- Salt and pepper to taste
- Lettuce leaves (such as iceberg or romaine) for wrapping

Instructions:
1. In a bowl, combine the drained tuna, diced avocado, mayonnaise, lemon juice, chopped red onion, chopped cilantro, salt, and pepper.
2. Mix well until all ingredients are combined and the mixture is creamy.
3. Taste and adjust seasonings as desired.
4. Spoon the tuna avocado mixture onto lettuce leaves.
5. Wrap the lettuce leaves around the filling to create lettuce wraps.
6. Serve and enjoy!

Nutrition Information (per serving):
- Calories: 350
- Protein: 30g
- Fat: 20g
- Carbohydrates: 12g
- fibre: 7g

RECIPE 12: PAN-SEARED HALIBUT WITH LEMON BUTTER SAUCE
Cooking Time: 15 minutes
Serves: 2
Ingredients:
- 2 halibut fillets (about 180g each)
- Salt and pepper to taste
- 2 tablespoons olive oil
- 2 tablespoons unsalted butter
- 2 cloves garlic, minced
- Juice of 1 lemon
- Fresh parsley, chopped (for garnish)
- Lemon wedges (for serving)

Instructions:
1. Season the halibut fillets with salt and pepper on both sides.
2. Heat olive oil in a skillet over medium-high heat.
3. Add the halibut fillets to the skillet and cook for 3-4 minutes on each side until golden brown and cooked through.
4. Remove the halibut fillets from the skillet and set aside.
5. In the same skillet, melt the butter over medium heat.
6. Add minced garlic and cook for 1 minute until fragrant.
7. Stir in the lemon juice and cook for another minute.
8. Return the halibut fillets to the skillet and spoon the lemon butter sauce over them.
9. Cook for an additional minute to heat through.
10. Garnish with fresh parsley and serve hot with lemon wedges.

Nutrition Information (per serving):
- Calories: 350
- Protein: 35g
- Fat: 22g
- Carbohydrates: 2g
- fibre: 0g

RECIPE 13: GLUTEN-FREE SHRIMP STIR-FRY

Cooking Time: 20 minutes
Serves: 4
Ingredients:

- 500g shrimp, peeled and deveined
- 2 tablespoons gluten-free soy sauce
- 1 tablespoon sesame oil
- 1 tablespoon honey
- 2 tablespoons olive oil
- 1 red bell pepper, sliced
- 1 yellow bell pepper, sliced
- 1 zucchini, sliced
- 1 carrot, julienned
- 2 cloves garlic, minced
- 1 tablespoon grated fresh ginger
- 2 green onions, chopped
- Sesame seeds (for garnish)
- Cooked rice or rice noodles (to serve)

Instructions:

1. In a bowl, combine gluten-free soy sauce, sesame oil, and honey. Mix well.
2. In a large skillet or wok, heat olive oil over medium-high heat.
3. Add minced garlic and grated ginger to the skillet and cook for 1 minute until fragrant.
4. Add the shrimp to the skillet and cook for 2-3 minutes until pink and cooked through.
5. Remove the shrimp from the skillet and set aside.
6. In the same skillet, add sliced bell peppers, zucchini, and julienned carrots. Stir-fry for 3-4 minutes until crisp-tender.
7. Return the cooked shrimp to the skillet and pour the soy sauce mixture over the ingredients. Stir to coat evenly.
8. Cook for another minute to heat through.
9. Sprinkle chopped green onions and sesame seeds over the stir-fry.
10. Serve hot over cooked rice or rice noodles.

Nutrition Information (per serving):

- Calories: 250
- Protein: 25g
- Fat: 10g
- Carbohydrates: 16g
- fibre: 3g

Note: As always, double-check the labels of ingredients to ensure they are gluten-free, and adjust the recipes according to your personal dietary needs and preferences. Enjoy your delicious gluten-free seafood meals!

Gluten-free side dish recipes

RECIPE 1: ROASTED GARLIC PARMESAN BRUSSELS SPROUTS

Cooking time: 25 minutes
Servings: 4
Ingredients:
- 500g Brussels sprouts
- 3 cloves garlic, minced
- 2 tablespoons olive oil
- 1/4 cup grated Parmesan cheese
- Salt and pepper to taste

Instructions:
1. Preheat your oven to 200°C/180°C fan/ Gas Mark 6.
2. Trim the ends of the Brussels sprouts and remove any outer leaves that are wilted or damaged. Cut them in half.
3. In a large bowl, toss the Brussels sprouts with minced garlic, olive oil, salt, and pepper until they are evenly coated.
4. Spread the Brussels sprouts in a single layer on a baking sheet lined with parchment paper.
5. Roast in the preheated oven for about 20-25 minutes, or until the Brussels sprouts are golden brown and tender.
6. Remove from the oven, sprinkle grated Parmesan cheese over the top, and toss to combine.
7. Serve immediately.

Nutrition information per serving:
- Calories: 165 kcal
- Carbohydrates: 13g
- Protein: 7g
- Fat: 11g
- fibre: 5g

RECIPE 2: LEMON GARLIC QUINOA

Cooking time: 20 minutes
Servings: 4
Ingredients:
- 200g quinoa
- 400ml vegetable broth
- Zest and juice of 1 lemon
- 2 cloves garlic, minced
- 2 tablespoons chopped fresh parsley
- Salt and pepper to taste

Instructions:
1. Rinse the quinoa under cold water in a fine-mesh sieve to remove any bitterness.
2. In a medium saucepan, bring the vegetable broth to a boil. Add the rinsed quinoa and reduce the heat to low. Cover and simmer for about 15-20 minutes, or until the quinoa is cooked and the liquid is absorbed.
3. In a small bowl, combine the lemon zest, lemon juice, minced garlic, chopped parsley, salt, and pepper.
4. Once the quinoa is cooked, remove it from the heat and let it sit covered for a few minutes.
5. Fluff the quinoa with a fork and then stir in the lemon-garlic mixture until well combined.
6. Taste and adjust the seasoning if needed.
7. Serve warm as a side dish.

Nutrition information per serving:
- Calories: 180 kcal
- Carbohydrates: 33g
- Protein: 6g
- Fat: 3g
- fibre: 4g

RECIPE 3: HONEY GLAZED CARROTS

Cooking time: 20 minutes
Servings: 4
Ingredients:
- 500g carrots, peeled and sliced into sticks
- 2 tablespoons unsalted butter
- 2 tablespoons honey
- 1 teaspoon fresh thyme leaves
- Salt and pepper to taste

Instructions:
1. In a large skillet or frying pan, melt the butter over medium heat.
2. Add the carrot sticks to the pan and sauté for about 5 minutes until they start to soften.
3. Drizzle the honey over the carrots and stir to coat them evenly.
4. Reduce the heat to low and cover the pan. Cook for an additional 10-15 minutes, or until the carrots are tender, stirring occasionally.
5. Sprinkle fresh thyme leaves, salt, and pepper over the carrots and stir to combine.
6. Cook for an additional 1-2 minutes to allow the flavours to meld.
7. Serve hot as a side dish.

Nutrition information per serving:
- Calories: 140 kcal
- Carbohydrates: 24g
- Protein: 1g
- Fat: 6g
- fibre: 4g

RECIPE 4: GARLIC PARMESAN QUINOA

Cooking time: 25 minutes
Servings: 4
Ingredients:
- 200g quinoa
- 400ml vegetable broth
- 2 tablespoons olive oil
- 3 cloves garlic, minced
- 1/4 cup grated Parmesan cheese
- 2 tablespoons chopped fresh parsley
- Salt and pepper to taste

Instructions:
1. Rinse the quinoa under cold water in a fine-mesh sieve.
2. In a medium saucepan, bring the vegetable broth to a boil. Add the rinsed quinoa and reduce the heat to low. Cover and simmer for about 15-20 minutes, or until the quinoa is cooked and the liquid is absorbed.
3. In a separate pan, heat the olive oil over medium heat. Add the minced garlic and sauté for 1-2 minutes until fragrant.
4. Add the cooked quinoa to the pan with the garlic and stir to combine.
5. Stir in the grated Parmesan cheese, chopped parsley, salt, and pepper. Cook for an additional 2-3 minutes until the cheese is melted and the flavors are well incorporated.
6. Remove from heat and let it sit covered for a few minutes.
7. Fluff the quinoa with a fork before serving.
8. Serve warm as a side dish.

Nutrition information per serving:
- Calories: 245 kcal
- Carbohydrates: 31g
- Protein: 8g
- Fat: 10g
- fibre: 4g

RECIPE 5: BALSAMIC ROASTED VEGETABLES

Cooking time: 30 minutes
Servings: 4
Ingredients:

- 2 medium courgettes, sliced
- 2 red bell peppers, seeded and sliced
- 1 red onion, sliced
- 250g cherry tomatoes
- 3 tablespoons balsamic vinegar
- 2 tablespoons olive oil
- 2 cloves garlic, minced
- 1 teaspoon dried oregano
- Salt and pepper to taste

Instructions:

1. Preheat your oven to 200°C/180°C fan/Gas Mark 6.
2. In a large bowl, combine the sliced courgettes, red bell peppers, red onion, and cherry tomatoes.
3. In a small bowl, whisk together balsamic vinegar, olive oil, minced garlic, dried oregano, salt, and pepper.
4. Pour the balsamic mixture over the vegetables and toss until they are well coated.
5. Spread the vegetables in a single layer on a baking sheet lined with parchment paper.
6. Roast in the preheated oven for about 25-30 minutes, stirring halfway through, until the vegetables are tender and caramelized.
7. Remove from the oven and let it cool slightly before serving.

Nutrition information per serving:

- Calories: 145 kcal
- Carbohydrates: 15g
- Protein: 3g
- Fat: 9g
- fibre: 4g

RECIPE 6: HERBED QUINOA SALAD

Cooking time: 25 minutes
Servings: 4
Ingredients:

- 200g quinoa
- 400ml vegetable broth
- 2 tablespoons olive oil
- Juice of 1 lemon
- 2 tablespoons chopped fresh parsley
- 1 tablespoon chopped fresh mint
- 1 tablespoon chopped fresh basil
- Salt and pepper to taste

Instructions:

1. Rinse the quinoa under cold water in a fine-mesh sieve.
2. In a medium saucepan, bring the vegetable broth to a boil. Add the rinsed quinoa and reduce the heat to low. Cover and simmer for about 15-20 minutes, or until the quinoa is cooked and the liquid is absorbed.
3. In a large bowl, combine the cooked quinoa, olive oil, lemon juice, chopped parsley, chopped mint, chopped basil, salt, and pepper. Toss until well combined.
4. Taste and adjust the seasoning if needed.
5. Allow the salad to cool slightly or refrigerate for a few minutes before serving.
6. Serve chilled or at room temperature.

Nutrition information per serving:

- Calories: 210 kcal
- Carbohydrates: 32g
- Protein: 6g
- Fat: 7g and fibre: 4g

RECIPE 7: ZUCCHINI FRITTERS

Cooking time: 20 minutes
Servings: 4
Ingredients:
- 2 medium zucchini
- 1 teaspoon salt
- 2 spring onions, finely chopped
- 2 cloves garlic, minced
- 1/4 cup gluten-free flour
- 1/4 cup grated Parmesan cheese
- 2 large eggs, beaten
- 2 tablespoons chopped fresh parsley
- 2 tablespoons olive oil
- Greek yogurt (optional, for serving)

Instructions:
1. Grate the zucchini using a box grater or food processor. Place the grated zucchini in a colander, sprinkle with salt, and let it sit for about 10 minutes to draw out the moisture.
2. Squeeze the excess liquid from the grated zucchini using your hands or a clean kitchen towel.
3. In a large bowl, combine the grated zucchini, spring onions, minced garlic, gluten-free flour, grated Parmesan cheese, beaten eggs, and chopped parsley. Mix well to form a thick batter.
4. Heat the olive oil in a non-stick frying pan over medium heat.
5. Drop spoonful's of the zucchini batter into the hot pan and flatten them slightly with the back of a spatula.
6. Cook the fritters for about 3-4 minutes on each side, or until they are golden brown and crispy.
7. Remove the fritters from the pan and drain on a paper towel.
8. Serve the zucchini fritters hot with a dollop of Greek yogurt, if desired.

Nutrition information per serving:
- Calories: 125 kcal
- Carbohydrates: 8g
- Protein: 7g
- Fat: 7g
- fibre: 2g

RECIPE 8: GARLIC ROASTED CAULIFLOWER

Cooking time: 25 minutes
Servings: 4
Ingredients:
- 1 large cauliflower, cut into florets
- 3 tablespoons olive oil
- 4 cloves garlic, minced
- 1 teaspoon smoked paprika
- 1/2 teaspoon ground cumin
- Salt and pepper to taste
- Fresh parsley, for garnish

Instructions:
1. Preheat your oven to 200°C/180°C fan/Gas Mark 6.
2. In a large bowl, combine the cauliflower florets, olive oil, minced garlic, smoked paprika, ground cumin, salt, and pepper. Toss until the cauliflower is well coated with the seasoning.
3. Spread the seasoned cauliflower in a single layer on a baking sheet lined with parchment paper.
4. Roast in the preheated oven for about 20-25 minutes, or until the cauliflower is tender and lightly browned, stirring halfway through.
5. Remove from the oven and garnish with fresh parsley.
6. Serve the garlic roasted cauliflower as a tasty side dish.

Nutrition information per serving:
- Calories: 120 kcal
- Carbohydrates: 9g
- Protein: 3g
- Fat: 9g and fibre: 4g

Recipe 9: Caprese Quinoa Salad
Cooking time: 20 minutes
Servings: 4
Ingredients:
- 200g quinoa
- 400ml vegetable broth
- 200g cherry tomatoes, halved
- 125g mozzarella cheese, diced
- 1/4 cup chopped fresh basil leaves
- 2 tablespoons olive oil
- 2 tablespoons balsamic vinegar
- Salt and pepper to taste

Instructions:
1. Rinse the quinoa under cold water in a fine-mesh sieve.
2. In a medium saucepan, bring the vegetable broth to a boil. Add the rinsed quinoa and reduce the heat to low. Cover and simmer for about 15-20 minutes, or until the quinoa is cooked and the liquid is absorbed.
3. In a large bowl, combine the cooked quinoa, cherry tomatoes, mozzarella cheese, and chopped basil leaves.
4. In a small bowl, whisk together the olive oil, balsamic vinegar, salt, and pepper.
5. Pour the dressing over the quinoa mixture and toss until well combined.
6. Taste and adjust the seasoning if needed.
7. Serve the Caprese quinoa salad at room temperature or chilled.

Nutrition information per serving:
- Calories: 300 kcal
- Carbohydrates: 35g
- Protein: 11g
- Fat: 13g
- fibre: 4g

RECIPE 10: SWEET POTATO WEDGES
Cooking time: 30 minutes
Servings: 4
Ingredients:
- 2 large sweet potatoes
- 2 tablespoons olive oil
- 1 teaspoon paprika
- 1/2 teaspoon garlic powder
- 1/2 teaspoon dried thyme
- 1/2 teaspoon salt
- 1/4 teaspoon black pepper
- Fresh parsley, for garnish

Instructions:
1. Preheat your oven to 220°C/200°C fan/Gas Mark 7.
2. Scrub the sweet potatoes clean and cut them into wedges.
3. In a large bowl, combine the olive oil, paprika, garlic powder, dried thyme, salt, and black pepper.
4. Add the sweet potato wedges to the bowl and toss until they are well coated with the seasoning mixture.
5. Arrange the seasoned sweet potato wedges in a single layer on a baking sheet lined with parchment paper.
6. Roast in the preheated oven for about 25-30 minutes, or until the sweet potatoes are tender and crispy, flipping them halfway through.
7. Remove from the oven and garnish with fresh parsley.
8. Serve the sweet potato wedges hot as a delicious side dish.

Nutrition information per serving:
- Calories: 180 kcal
- Carbohydrates: 27g

- Protein: 2g
- Fat: 8g
- fibre: 4g

RECIPE 11: LEMON HERB ROASTED POTATOES

Cooking time: 40 minutes
Servings: 4
Ingredients:
- 800g baby potatoes, halved
- 3 tablespoons olive oil
- 2 tablespoons lemon juice
- 2 cloves garlic, minced
- 1 tablespoon chopped fresh rosemary
- 1 tablespoon chopped fresh thyme
- Salt and pepper to taste

Instructions:
1. Preheat your oven to 200°C/180°C fan/Gas Mark 6.
2. In a large bowl, combine the halved baby potatoes, olive oil, lemon juice, minced garlic, chopped rosemary, chopped thyme, salt, and pepper. Toss until the potatoes are well coated with the mixture.
3. Spread the seasoned potatoes in a single layer on a baking sheet lined with parchment paper.
4. Roast in the preheated oven for about 35-40 minutes, or until the potatoes are golden brown and crispy, stirring occasionally for even cooking.
5. Remove from the oven and serve the lemon herb roasted potatoes hot as a delightful side dish.

Nutrition information per serving:
- Calories: 210 kcal
- Carbohydrates: 30g
- Protein: 3g
- Fat: 9g
- fibre: 3g

RECIPE 12: GRILLED ASPARAGUS WITH LEMON AND PARMESAN

Cooking time: 15 minutes
Servings: 4
Ingredients:
- 400g asparagus spears, trimmed
- 2 tablespoons olive oil
- Zest and juice of 1 lemon
- 2 tablespoons grated Parmesan cheese
- Salt and pepper to taste

Instructions:
1. Preheat your grill or grill pan over medium-high heat.
2. In a shallow dish, combine the asparagus spears, olive oil, lemon zest, lemon juice, grated Parmesan cheese, salt, and pepper. Toss until the asparagus is evenly coated.
3. Place the asparagus spears on the grill and cook for about 5-7 minutes, turning occasionally, until they are tender and charred in spots.
4. Remove the grilled asparagus from the heat and transfer them to a serving platter.
5. Sprinkle with additional grated Parmesan cheese and serve immediately.

Nutrition information per serving:
- Calories: 85 kcal
- Carbohydrates: 5g
- Protein: 4g
- Fat: 6g
- fibre: 2g

RECIPE 13: CUCUMBER TOMATO SALAD

Cooking time: 10 minutes
Servings: 4
Ingredients:
- 2 cucumbers, sliced
- 250g cherry tomatoes, halved
- 1/4 red onion, thinly sliced
- 2 tablespoons chopped fresh dill
- 2 tablespoons olive oil
- 1 tablespoon red wine vinegar
- Salt and pepper to taste

Instructions:
1. In a large bowl, combine the sliced cucumbers, cherry tomatoes, red onion, and chopped fresh dill.
2. In a small bowl, whisk together the olive oil, red wine vinegar, salt, and pepper.
3. Pour the dressing over the cucumber mixture and toss until well coated.
4. Taste and adjust the seasoning if needed.
5. Serve the cucumber tomato salad chilled as a refreshing side dish.

Nutrition information per serving:
- Calories: 85 kcal
- Carbohydrates: 6g
- Protein: 1g
- Fat: 7g
- fibre: 1g

RECIPE 14: ROASTED GARLIC CAULIFLOWER MASH

Cooking time: 30 minutes
Servings: 4
Ingredients:
- 1 large head of cauliflower, cut into florets
- 4 cloves garlic, peeled
- 2 tablespoons olive oil
- 1/4 cup unsweetened almond milk (or any other milk alternative)
- 2 tablespoons dairy-free butter
- Salt and pepper to taste
- Chopped fresh chives, for garnish

Instructions:
1. Preheat your oven to 200°C/180°C fan/Gas Mark 6.
2. Place the cauliflower florets and peeled garlic cloves on a baking sheet. Drizzle with olive oil and toss to coat.
3. Roast in the preheated oven for about 20-25 minutes, or until the cauliflower is tender and lightly browned, and the garlic is softened.
4. Transfer the roasted cauliflower and garlic to a food processor or blender.
5. Add almond milk, dairy-free butter, salt, and pepper to the food processor. Process until smooth and creamy.
6. Taste and adjust the seasoning if needed.
7. Transfer the cauliflower mash to a serving bowl and garnish with chopped fresh chives.
8. Serve the roasted garlic cauliflower mash hot as a delicious side dish.

Nutrition information per serving:
- Calories: 90 kcal
- Carbohydrates: 8g
- Protein: 3g
- Fat: 6g
- fibre: 3g

RECIPE 15: BAKED PARMESAN ZUCCHINI FRIES

Cooking time: 25 minutes
Servings: 4
Ingredients:

- 2 medium zucchini
- 1/2 cup grated Parmesan cheese
- 1/2 cup gluten-free breadcrumbs
- 1 teaspoon garlic powder
- 1/2 teaspoon dried oregano
- 1/2 teaspoon paprika
- Salt and pepper to taste
- 2 large eggs, beaten
- Cooking spray

Instructions:

1. Preheat your oven to 220°C/200°C fan/Gas Mark 7. Line a baking sheet with parchment paper and lightly coat it with cooking spray.
2. Cut the zucchini into long strips, resembling fries.
3. In a shallow dish, combine the grated Parmesan cheese, gluten-free breadcrumbs, garlic powder, dried oregano, paprika, salt, and pepper.
4. Dip each zucchini strip into the beaten eggs and then coat it with the Parmesan mixture, pressing gently to adhere.
5. Place the coated zucchini strips on the prepared baking sheet in a single layer.
6. Bake in the preheated oven for about 20-25 minutes, or until the zucchini fries are golden brown and crispy.
7. Serve the baked Parmesan zucchini fries hot as a delicious side dish.

Nutrition information per serving:

- Calories: 130 kcal
- Carbohydrates: 9g
- Protein: 9g
- Fat: 7g
- fibre: 2g

Gluten-Free Vegetable Recipes

Recipe 1: Roasted Garlic and Herb Cauliflower Rice

Cooking Time: 25 minutes
Serves: 4
Ingredients:
- 1 medium head cauliflower
- 2 tablespoons olive oil
- 4 cloves garlic, minced
- 1 teaspoon dried mixed herbs
- Salt and pepper to taste

Instructions:
1. Preheat the oven to 200°C (180°C fan-assisted). Line a baking sheet with parchment paper.
2. Cut the cauliflower into florets and pulse in a food processor until it reaches a rice-like consistency.
3. In a large bowl, combine the cauliflower rice, olive oil, minced garlic, dried herbs, salt, and pepper. Mix well to evenly coat the cauliflower.
4. Spread the cauliflower rice mixture onto the prepared baking sheet, ensuring it forms a single layer.
5. Roast in the preheated oven for 20 minutes, or until the cauliflower rice is tender and slightly golden, stirring halfway through.
6. Remove from the oven and serve as a side dish or as a base for your favourite stir-fries or curries.

Nutrition Information per Serving:
- Calories: 86 kcal
- Protein: 3g
- Carbohydrates: 8g
- Fat: 5g
- fibre: 3g

Recipe 2: Zucchini Noodles with Tomato and Basil

Cooking Time: 20 minutes
Serves: 2
Ingredients:
- 2 medium zucchini
- 2 tablespoons olive oil
- 2 cloves garlic, minced
- 200g cherry tomatoes, halved
- 1 tablespoon balsamic vinegar
- Fresh basil leaves, chopped
- Salt and pepper to taste

Instructions:
1. Spiralized the zucchini into noodle-like strands using a spiralized or julienne peeler. Set aside.
2. Heat the olive oil in a large pan over medium heat. Add the minced garlic and sauté until fragrant.
3. Add the cherry tomatoes to the pan and cook for 5 minutes, or until they start to soften.
4. Stir in the zucchini noodles and cook for an additional 3-4 minutes, until they are just tender.
5. Drizzle the balsamic vinegar over the noodles and toss to combine.
6. Season with salt and pepper to taste.
7. Remove from heat, garnish with fresh basil leaves, and serve immediately.

Nutrition Information per Serving:
- Calories: 152 kcal
- Protein: 3g

- Carbohydrates: 10g
- Fat: 12g
- fibre: 3g

RECIPE 3: SWEET POTATO AND CHICKPEA CURRY

Cooking Time: 30 minutes
Serves: 4
Ingredients:

- 2 tablespoons coconut oil
- 1 large onion, diced
- 3 cloves garlic, minced
- 1 tablespoon fresh ginger, grated
- 2 medium sweet potatoes, peeled and cubed
- 1 can (400g) chickpeas, drained and rinsed
- 1 can (400ml) coconut milk
- 2 tablespoons curry powder
- 1 teaspoon turmeric
- Salt and pepper to taste
- Fresh cilantro leaves, chopped (for garnish)

Instructions:

1. Heat the coconut oil in a large pan over medium heat. Add the diced onion and sauté until translucent.
2. Add the minced garlic and grated ginger to the pan, and cook for an additional minute.
3. Stir in the sweet potatoes, chickpeas, coconut milk, curry powder, and turmeric. Season with salt and pepper.
4. Bring the mixture to a simmer and let it cook for about 20 minutes, or until the sweet potatoes are tender.
5. Serve the curry hot, garnished with fresh cilantro leaves, over steamed rice or with gluten-free naan bread.

Nutrition Information per Serving:

- Calories: 347 kcal
- Protein: 8g
- Carbohydrates: 39g
- Fat: 19g
- fibre: 8g

RECIPE 4: SPINACH AND MUSHROOM QUINOA STIR-FRY

Cooking Time: 25 minutes
Serves: 2
Ingredients:

- 1 cup quinoa
- 2 cups vegetable broth
- 2 tablespoons olive oil
- 1 small onion, diced
- 2 cloves garlic, minced
- 200g mushrooms, sliced
- 4 cups fresh spinach leaves
- 2 tablespoons gluten-free soy sauce
- 1 teaspoon sesame oil
- Salt and pepper to taste

Instructions:

1. Rinse the quinoa under cold water. In a saucepan, bring the vegetable broth to a boil, then add the quinoa. Reduce the heat, cover, and let it simmer for about 15 minutes, or until the quinoa is cooked and the broth is absorbed.
2. In a large pan, heat the olive oil over medium heat. Add the diced onion and minced garlic, and sauté until the onion becomes translucent.
3. Add the sliced mushrooms to the pan and cook for about 5 minutes, or until they start to brown.
4. Stir in the fresh spinach leaves and cook until wilted.

5. Add the cooked quinoa to the pan and mix well to combine.
6. Drizzle gluten-free soy sauce and sesame oil over the stir-fry. Season with salt and pepper to taste.
7. Cook for an additional 2-3 minutes, stirring occasionally.
8. Remove from heat and serve hot.

Nutrition Information per Serving:
- Calories: 396 kcal
- Protein: 13g
- Carbohydrates: 56g
- Fat: 15g
- fibre: 9g

RECIPE 5: OVEN-ROASTED ROOT VEGETABLES
Cooking Time: 30 minutes
Serves: 4
Ingredients:
- 2 medium carrots, peeled and cut into chunks
- 2 medium parsnips, peeled and cut into chunks
- 1 medium beetroot, peeled and cut into chunks
- 1 medium sweet potato, peeled and cut into chunks
- 2 tablespoons olive oil
- 1 teaspoon dried thyme
- 1 teaspoon dried rosemary
- Salt and pepper to taste

Instructions:
1. Preheat the oven to 200°C (180°C fan-assisted). Line a baking sheet with parchment paper.
2. In a large bowl, combine the carrot chunks, parsnip chunks, beetroot chunks, and sweet potato chunks.
3. Drizzle olive oil over the vegetables and toss to coat them evenly.
4. Sprinkle dried thyme, dried rosemary, salt, and pepper over the vegetables. Mix well.
5. Spread the seasoned vegetables onto the prepared baking sheet in a single layer.
6. Roast in the preheated oven for 25-30 minutes, or until the vegetables are tender and slightly caramelized, stirring halfway through.
7. Remove from the oven and serve as a side dish or as a filling for gluten-free wraps or salads.

Nutrition Information per Serving:
- Calories: 169 kcal
- Protein: 2g
- Carbohydrates: 28g
- Fat: 6g
- fibre: 6g

RECIPE 6: CAPRESE STUFFED PORTOBELLO MUSHROOMS
Cooking Time: 25 minutes
Serves: 2
Ingredients:
- 2 large Portobello mushrooms
- 2 tablespoons olive oil
- 2 cloves garlic, minced
- 4 slices mozzarella cheese
- 2 medium tomatoes, sliced
- Fresh basil leaves
- Balsamic glaze (for drizzling)
- Salt and pepper to taste

Instructions:
1. Preheat the oven to 200°C (180°C fan-assisted). Line a baking sheet with parchment paper.
2. Clean the Portobello mushrooms and remove the stems.

3. In a small bowl, combine the olive oil and minced garlic. Brush the mixture over the mushrooms, coating both sides.
4. Place the mushrooms on the prepared baking sheet and season with salt and pepper.
5. Bake in the preheated oven for 10 minutes.
6. Remove the mushrooms from the oven and top each mushroom with a slice of mozzarella cheese.
7. Add tomato slices on top of the cheese and return to the oven for an additional 10 minutes, or until the cheese is melted and bubbly.
8. Remove from the oven, garnish with fresh basil leaves, and drizzle with balsamic glaze.
9. Serve hot as a main course or alongside a salad.

Nutrition Information per Serving:
- Calories: 285 kcal
- Protein: 14g
- Carbohydrates: 8g
- Fat: 22g
- fibre: 2g

RECIPE 7: RAINBOW VEGGIE STIR-FRY

Cooking Time: 20 minutes
Serves: 4
Ingredients:
- 1 red bell pepper, thinly sliced
- 1 yellow bell pepper, thinly sliced
- 1 orange bell pepper, thinly sliced
- 1 small zucchini, thinly sliced
- 1 small yellow squash, thinly sliced
- 1 cup sugar snaps peas
- 2 tablespoons gluten-free soy sauce
- 1 tablespoon sesame oil
- 1 tablespoon rice vinegar
- 1 tablespoon honey
- 2 cloves garlic, minced
- 1 teaspoon grated ginger
- 2 tablespoons olive oil
- Sesame seeds (for garnish)
- Salt and pepper to taste

Instructions:
1. In a small bowl, whisk together the gluten-free soy sauce, sesame oil, rice vinegar, honey, minced garlic, and grated ginger. Set aside.
2. Heat the olive oil in a large pan or wok over medium-high heat.
3. Add the bell peppers, zucchini, yellow squash, and sugar snap peas to the pan. Stir-fry for 4-5 minutes, or until the vegetables are crisp-tender.
4. Pour the prepared sauce over the vegetables and stir well to coat.
5. Continue to cook for an additional 2-3 minutes, until the sauce thickens slightly.
6. Season with salt and pepper to taste.
7. Remove from heat and garnish with sesame seeds.
8. Serve hot as a side dish or over steamed rice or gluten-free noodles.

Nutrition Information per Serving:
- Calories: 118 kcal
- Protein: 3g
- Carbohydrates: 12g
- Fat: 8g
- fibre: 3g

RECIPE 8: CHICKPEA AND VEGETABLE CURRY

Cooking Time: 25 minutes
Serves: 4
Ingredients:

- 1 tablespoon coconut oil
- 1 medium onion, diced
- 2 cloves garlic, minced
- 1 tablespoon fresh ginger, grated
- 1 red bell pepper, diced
- 1 medium carrot, diced
- 1 medium zucchini, diced
- 1 can (400g) diced tomatoes
- 1 can (400ml) coconut milk
- 2 teaspoons curry powder
- 1 teaspoon ground cumin
- 1 teaspoon ground coriander
- 1 can (400g) chickpeas, drained and rinsed
- Fresh cilantro leaves, chopped (for garnish)
- Salt and pepper to taste

Instructions:

1. Heat the coconut oil in a large pan over medium heat. Add the diced onion and sauté until translucent.
2. Add the minced garlic and grated ginger to the pan, and cook for an additional minute.
3. Add the diced bell pepper, carrot, and zucchini to the pan. Sauté for 5 minutes, or until the vegetables start to soften.
4. Stir in the diced tomatoes, coconut milk, curry powder, ground cumin, and ground coriander. Season with salt and pepper.
5. Bring the mixture to a simmer and let it cook for about 10 minutes, allowing the flavors to meld together.
6. Add the chickpeas to the pan and cook for an additional 5 minutes, until heated through.
7. Remove from heat and garnish with fresh cilantro leaves.
8. Serve hot over steamed rice or with gluten-free naan bread.

Nutrition Information per Serving:

- Calories: 292 kcal
- Protein: 10g
- Carbohydrates: 34g
- Fat: 14g
- fibre: 9g

RECIPE 9: ROASTED BRUSSELS SPROUTS WITH BALSAMIC GLAZE

Cooking Time: 25 minutes
Serves: 4
Ingredients:

- 500g Brussels sprouts, trimmed and halved
- 2 tablespoons olive oil
- 2 tablespoons balsamic vinegar
- 1 tablespoon honey
- Salt and pepper to taste

Instructions:

1. Preheat the oven to 200°C (180°C fan-assisted). Line a baking sheet with parchment paper.
2. In a large bowl, toss the Brussels sprouts with olive oil, balsamic vinegar, honey, salt, and pepper until evenly coated.
3. Spread the Brussels sprouts onto the prepared baking sheet in a single layer.
4. Roast in the preheated oven for 20-25 minutes, or until the Brussels sprouts are tender and caramelized, stirring halfway through.
5. Remove from the oven and let them cool for a few minutes.

6. Serve as a side dish or as a delicious addition to salads or grain bowls.

Nutrition Information per Serving:
- Calories: 110 kcal
- Protein: 4g
- Carbohydrates: 15g
- Fat: 5g
- fibre: 5g

RECIPE 10: QUINOA STUFFED BELL PEPPERS
Cooking Time: 35 minutes
Serves: 4
Ingredients:
- 4 large bell peppers (any colour)
- 1 cup cooked quinoa
- 1 small onion, diced
- 2 cloves garlic, minced
- 1 medium zucchini, diced
- 1 medium carrot, grated
- 1 cup canned black beans, drained and rinsed
- 1 cup diced tomatoes
- 1 teaspoon dried oregano
- 1 teaspoon ground cumin
- Salt and pepper to taste
- Olive oil (for drizzling)

Instructions:
1. Preheat the oven to 180°C (160°C fan-assisted). Cut off the tops of the bell peppers and remove the seeds and membranes.
2. In a large pan, heat some olive oil over medium heat. Add the diced onion and minced garlic, and sauté until the onion becomes translucent.
3. Add the diced zucchini and grated carrot to the pan, and cook for about 5 minutes, or until the vegetables start to soften.
4. Stir in the cooked quinoa, black beans, diced tomatoes, dried oregano, ground cumin, salt, and pepper. Mix well.
5. Stuff the bell peppers with the quinoa and vegetable mixture, pressing it down to fill the peppers completely.
6. Place the stuffed bell peppers upright in a baking dish. Drizzle a little olive oil over the top of each pepper.
7. Bake in the preheated oven for 25-30 minutes, or until the bell peppers are tender and slightly charred.
8. Remove from the oven and let them cool for a few minutes before serving.

Nutrition Information per Serving:
- Calories: 231 kcal
- Protein: 10g
- Carbohydrates: 45g
- Fat: 2g
- Fiber: 11g

RECIPE 11: GARLIC HERB ROASTED VEGETABLES

Cooking Time: 30 minutes
Serves: 4
Ingredients:

- 1 medium butternut squash, peeled, seeded, and cut into cubes
- 2 medium carrots, peeled and cut into chunks
- 2 medium parsnips, peeled and cut into chunks
- 1 red onion, cut into wedges
- 2 tablespoons olive oil
- 4 cloves garlic, minced
- 1 teaspoon dried thyme
- 1 teaspoon dried rosemary
- Salt and pepper to taste

Instructions:
1. Preheat the oven to 200°C (180°C fan-assisted). Line a baking sheet with parchment paper.
2. In a large bowl, combine the butternut squash cubes, carrot chunks, parsnip chunks, and red onion wedges.
3. Drizzle olive oil over the vegetables and toss to coat them evenly.
4. Add the minced garlic, dried thyme, dried rosemary, salt, and pepper. Mix well.
5. Spread the seasoned vegetables onto the prepared baking sheet in a single layer.
6. Roast in the preheated oven for 25-30 minutes, or until the vegetables are tender and caramelized, stirring halfway through.
7. Remove from the oven and serve as a side dish or as a filling for gluten-free wraps or salads.

Nutrition Information per Serving:

- Calories: 186 kcal
- Protein: 3g
- Carbohydrates: 34g
- Fat: 7g
- fibre: 8g

Enjoy these additional gluten-free vegetable recipes!